Praise for G
T0168338

"Each story is entertaining and exciting."
North American Bear Foundation

"Reed writes with compassion for bears and their struggle to inhabit 'the last few kernels we are leaving them.'"
High Country News

"Tom Reed's book is a wonderful collection of stories about bears, bear encounters, and bear attacks in Wyoming. If you live in this region, or you like exploring the backcountry, you should buy this book."
Yellowstone Journal

"One finds a compendium of well-written and deeply researched, yet no-less-gripping tales of the Cowboy State's black bears and grizzlies."
The Daily Sentinel

"Tom Reed may have a hit with his first book."
Casper Star Tribune

Great Wyoming

BEAR

STORIES

Tom Reed

Riverbend Publishing

ISBN 1-931832-30-7

Cover design by Julie Darby, Black Dog Design, Lander, Wyoming
Text design by Suzan Glosser, Riverbend Publishing

Front cover photos:
    Grizzly bear by Michael H. Francis.
    Historic photo: "Our First Grizzly, killed by Gen. Custer and
        Col. Ludlow." By Illingworth, 1874, during the Black Hills
        Expedition. Courtesy of the National Archives.

Back cover photo:
    Black bear by Michael H. Francis.

Grizzly track illustrations by Joan M. Safford.

Riverbend Publishing
P.O. Box 5833
Helena, MT 59604
1-866-787-2363
www.riverbendpublishing.com

*To wild country and wild bears
and those who find value in both.*

Acknowledgments

Behind every writer, there's an outstanding researcher or two and I am indebted to a few. I am particularly grateful to Alissa Cherry at the Yellowstone Research Library, Joseph Schwarz at the National Archives, and Venice Beske at the Wyoming State Library. Without these people doing the digging, there wouldn't have been much to tell.

I also owe my friends Mark Bruscino, Jay Lawson, and Jerry Longobardi at the Wyoming Game and Fish Department more than a couple of beers. Wyoming is lucky to employ some of the best wildlife professionals in the world and these guys stand at the top for their dedication to wildlife and wild places. They and other wardens and biologists help make Wyoming the wonderful place that it is. The incomparable editor of *Wyoming Wildlife* magazine, Chris Madson, is among the elite as well and I thank him in particular for making this book happen by putting publisher Chris Cauble in touch with me in the first place. Thanks Chris and Chris.

A special acknowledgement goes out to my hunting buddies, the Glenn brothers, who, along with their dad, Bob, define what it means to be an outdoorsman and a conservationist. These days hunters and conservationists are separated into two different categories, which is a sad commentary for the future of wild country. Men like Teddy Roosevelt and Aldo Leopold knew that hunter means conservationist and conservationist means hunter. The Glenns are of that ilk and I'm proud to be part of their hunting camp each fall. All too seldom, another great conservationist (read hunter) joins us from his home outside Silver Star, Montana. Jim Houston has been a friend, mentor, and model of hunting ethics in my life. I'm grateful for his friendship and the use of his world-class outdoor library.

Thanks go out to Kathleen Raymond, Tiffany Meredith, and Janet Milek for reading the manuscript before it hit the streets, and particularly Patricia Dowd for her encouragement, proofreading ability, and support.

I also want to thank everyone who shared their time and stories with me. I interviewed dozens of people who have visited bear country, lived in bear country, and been changed by bear country. Their stories are inspiring and captivating. I hope I captured the essence.

Several years ago, illustrator Joan Safford and I stood on the banks of the upper Yellowstone River and read the tale of a grizzly bear on the river's pages. Thanks to Joan for her deftness with the sketchpad, and to designer and long-time colleague Julie Darby for putting it all together for the bookshelf.

Thanks go out to my parents, Chuck and Virginia Reed, for providing me with the opportunity to get outside and to the memory of Helen Waters for her love of the written word.

Contents

Introduction: In his country

September 2002, Somewhere in the Absaroka Mountains, Wyoming

"Uh-oh."

There is no mistaking the words. Dave is standing on a slight rise of forest floor looking down into a shallow ravine. I cannot see what he is looking at, but I can definitely feel the tension in his voice. "Uh-oh" means bear. Immediately I start talking a bit louder—but not shouting—steady and very audible, "Hey bear, hey bear. We are just walking through the woods. Hey bear."

It is one of those frozen moments when time seems to inch by but reality is a flash. Somewhere far off, a bird calls, a squirrel barks. My heart gallops. A second earlier we were full of ourselves, full of success, enjoying the moment. Now, everything, every sense, is on high alert. *Alive.* The bear spray that was on my hip is in my hand. I don't remember how it got there.

We are in dark, thick timber, walking single file. Dave is leading, followed by me and then Al. We smell of game, of blood and meat and mule deer. We are carrying portions of the freshly killed mule deer buck that I've shot. The quarters are slung over our shoulders. We were talking and we were laughing, but now we are not. We are making noise, but this is not the noise of happy successful hunters on their way downhill to the horses and camp. Now the echoes of our voices in the thick Englemann spruce carry words that we hope the bear understands, somehow. We are not out to hurt him or steal his food; we ask only a modest and temporary trespass through his home.

We have just walked—laughing and talking—but walked nevertheless, to within twenty yards of the bear's cached carcass of an elk.

There, in a perfectly sculpted mound of pine needles, is the clear outline of a bull elk. We know it is a bull because the antlers stick out of the mound. Were it not for those antlers, we might have walked right past that elk without knowing it was even there. But perhaps not. The outline is perfect, natural somehow, as if the bear has an artistic side and sculpts in forest duff rather than clay or stone. It is an elk made not of flesh and blood and bone but of pine needle and twig. He is the earth, not of it.

We theorize this bull was shot and wounded up-country by a piss-poor marksman from the outfitter's camp down the valley. We heard the shooting opening morning. Five, ten, twelve shots fired in rapid succession. We cursed those who cannot shoot, who don't care enough to make a shot that counts the first time.

We mourn for an elk that probably died a painful death, shot perhaps in the gut or hindquarters, but the elk was not wasted. Nothing is wasted. The elk will feed the bear instead of the man who shot him so poorly. Slowly, grateful that the bear has not charged us off of his find, we back out of there, trying to look in every direction. We will try another route down off the steep canyon. We have bear spray, we have firearms, and we are three. We never see the bear.

September 1999, Elk Camp, Teton Wilderness, Wyoming

That first night he comes into the meadow. We see the horses lift their heads from the grass. We see all six stand straight and tall, ears perked forward, missing nothing. The bay traveling mare is closest and she is balanced. One year she had a mature bull moose come grunting to within ten feet of her while she grazed calmly at the end of her picket rope. Whatever the bull was telling the mare didn't work, for she simply ignored him. The younger horses will follow her lead. If she is calm, they are calm; if she spooks, they will spook. They are alert, not alarmed.

We walk to the edge of the timber from our cook tent, plates of forgotten food in our hands, and we watch him walk in the meadow, heading down-country in the farewell light of another mountain day. Going somewhere. The horses don't care. Perhaps their hearts race like ours, but perhaps not.

We say nothing. The big grizzly knows we are here for he is only about 150 yards out, crossing the meadow, moving into the timber and toward the trail we rode this afternoon. Occasionally his head pendulums our way. We have firearms and bear spray, but there is no mad dash for either. He is not bothering us. It is enough just to watch him, to watch the angled, orange sunlight of fading day shine on his hide, to watch how he moves, how his fur ripples. It is enough. In fact it is reward, payment for all the hard work we did packing elk camp to this spot we call—all too seldom and all too briefly—ours. But it really is his. We are guests in his house.

That night he comes back and rattles about in our cook area. We hear him, but we have stashed everything away, hung things in trees, and locked things in bear-proof panniers. We are sleeping well away from our dining room, and everything, even the tiniest trace of pasta, even toothpaste and lip balm, has been put out of bear reach. Bear proofed. How, we think, could one come into someone else's home and act like a slob?

We call out into the night and we rise. It is near dawn and there's a thread of light on the horizon, promising day. We walk toward the kitchen area with bear spray drawn in one hand, a firearm in the other, but he has gone. He has knocked over our tack pile and left his teeth marks on one of the saddles. You can see the canines there, deeply scarring the leather, a bite as if to say, okay, you are in my living room, but keep it clean, damnit!

For a week, ten days, we hunt elk. He walks the trail behind our camp every morning. We see his tracks there, deep in the mud. And for a week, he leaves us alone. He has gotten no food reward, and somehow, we feel as if he understands that we are just here for the country, for the elk, for a short moment of decompression.

And we are here for him. There are tamer mountains, but they are merely mountains. He is wilderness, wilderness is him.

July 1998, Fox Park, Teton Wilderness, Wyoming

I call them The Boys and we have entered into a partnership, these two horses and I. They are bays, both are marked exactly the same though one is a shade lighter than the other. They each have a star of white on the forehead. It is their only white mark. Their legs are as straight and true and dark as a fire-blackened lodgepole. They carry me and they carry my food and that is all I can ask of them. In return, I take care of them and let them graze tall grass in far-back meadows and drink cold water from mountain streams. I feed them oats each night and place my open palm on their necks and I tell them stories of the grass and the water ahead. I think they know. It is the ideal partnership.

I carry no gun. I carry only the responsibility of eight young women and men who look to me for leadership, for knowledge. I'm teaching them how to horsepack and they are doing well. Some have never ridden, but after a week, two weeks, three weeks, they will be packers. We ride.

Deep into it, well back into the tall uncut, we pitch camp at the edge of a vast valley called Fox Park. It is here that the trip sinks into our souls. It is summer and after we turn The Boys and the rest of the gang out into the meadow, after they are hobbled and belled and picketed, we lean back on elbows in tall grass and swat the occasional mosquito. We are sated in that feeling that only comes with hard work and saddle time, with mountains and creeks and wildflowers growing in damp corners of wilderness meadow.

She arrives without announcement, as you'd expect her to arrive. She has a cub, a cub of the year, and it sprints past her and then stops. She gains on it and passes, and the cub sprints past and stops. It goes on and we watch. We were talking about something funny or important, or unimportant, but whatever it was, it flies out of our minds. Everyone watches as the sow grizzly moves far out in the park, right in the middle of it. She stops and digs occasionally, then moves on, heading northwest toward Yellowstone National Park, her cub shadowing and sprinting forward, moving, moving. And then gone.

We ride for another week, up into some of the finest country left on this planet. We ride to the sound of waterfall and river in narrow valleys that perhaps see only a half dozen people each year. We ride, but even though we leave that sow and her cub far back in Fox Park, she stays with us. At the end, I ask my horsepackers what they thought of the trip, what memory clings tight and will be remembered long after all the hard work has faded from tight muscle. It is unanimous. It is her.

September 1995, Secret Peak, Wyoming

The memory of elk pulls us up the mountain. It is a classic piece of elk country. There are wallows at its toe, among the alpine fir and monkeyflowers, places where a big bull has thrashed about in cool mud, has dug the polished tips of his antlers into the soil and raked bare the limbs of hapless whitebark pine. We find these places of chaos and lust, places that make our skin tingle, places that look as if they were frequented by something strange and primitive and savage. We find these places where sap and mud bleeds from fresh wounds. They are fresh signs, so new that the sap still drips and the mud hangs suspended in shallow, milk-chocolate pools.

The open ridge where the elk were last year is above us and slightly north. If the elk are there this year, we will plan a stalk, edging our boots precariously into the steep, touchy ravines and climbing sun-charred grass and wildflower, working down and up, rising and falling and always aware of the wind and its flow.

We work high on the ridge, up through the whitebark pine and its swollen purple cones, holding our rifles, breathing through our noses when we can, through our mouths when the air comes thin and fine. The last pitch takes us to a knife-edge of whitebark where we can get a view of the far ridge. The elk ridge. We hope to find the elk herd there this year, as if elk are such creatures of habit that they will appear every year in exactly the same place, in almost exactly the same footprints. It is a shallow wish, but it is vapors of promise that drive a hunter's heart.

The ridge does not disappoint but it is not elk. Instead it is *grizz*. The naked eye sweeps the ridge and immediately picks them up, dark moving spots of bear hide, not the creamed-coffee rumps of herded elk. And so we sit back, our packs still on, leveraging ourselves against them, binoculars to our eyes and we watch. There are four bears and they move and feed. We think they are feeding on the whitebark pine, but more likely they are feeding on anything that is edible, including the whitebark. A sow and a yearling cub. Perhaps a sub-adult and a bigger bear that could be a female without cubs, or a male. Not a huge old boar, but still, a bigger bear. We watch. We tied the horses far below, 1,000 feet or more down the mountain. It was a climb of sweat and bunched muscle, of pounding heart and pumping lung. The muscle memory of the climb fades, but our hearts still hammer, our breath is still shallow.

Why, one might ask, do you hunt elk in such a place as this? Why do you tread the same soil as *Ursus arctos*? (It's politically correct these days to leave the *horribilis* off the end, but his full name is *Ursus arctos horribilis*.) Don't you know there are plenty of elk and deer and moose somewhere else where there aren't any damned grizzlies?

We cannot help ourselves, for something pulls us there. Perhaps when you yourself are potential prey, it is easier to think like prey. It's less of a leap, maybe, from thinking like prey when you are prey, to thinking like prey when you are a predator. But perhaps it isn't nearly as profound as all this. Perhaps it's about living. More accurately, about being alive.

Maybe it's about being wild and in this tamed-out and roaded-up world, we seldom get close to that wildness, that true rawness. The Spanish philosopher, Jose Ortega y Gasset, called it "the savage man."

It's about being down a link on the food chain. It's about being in a place where every step is taken with great care. More than anything, it's about respect, for quarry, for man, for camp, for wilderness, for equine, for bear.

September 1968, Waugh Mountain, Colorado

In this land there is a whisper of a legend of a great bear. That bear was Old Mose, a cattle killer, a sheep killer, reputed to be a man killer. All is no doubt exaggerated, blown out of proportion, twisted by time and tale, legend and myth.

The land has been cleaned, homogenized, and hermetically sealed for our protection. There are no grizzlies here. It's been six decades since grizzlies prowled this country, since Old Mose walked across the big empty between Waugh and Black and Thirty-Nine Mile mountains, since he supped on lamb and veal. Now there is only whisper and fable. But even now the land holds his tale, as if the two cannot be torn apart, cannot exist without the other.

The lore is enough to capture the heart of a six-year-old boy, legend that is told to the boy by his grandmother, who lives on this wide fine place with its aspens and Douglas-fir and its views of Pike's Peak far to the east. The boy walks the land and thinks of bears. He sees the tracks of black bears and dreams that he has actually seen bears, although he never has. He reads their marks on the paper of the aspens, claw marks that are old and are now part of the history of the tree. Once, long ago, a mother bear told her cub to climb this aspen and the cub did, all the way, fifty or sixty feet up. The cub left his mark up and down the tree and the black scars on white bark will not be erased until the tree dies and the bark peels and falls in a winter storm and the tree follows a year or two later. But the story of the bear is the story of the tree and both become the story of the boy.

There are stories of bears in these pages. But there are stories of people as well. There cannot be one without the other; there cannot be stories without someone to do the telling and someone to do the listening.

Wyoming is bear country. Most of it, even out in the basins where narrow green threads of cottonwood and willow follow the drainages, is used or has been used by bears. The black bear lives in most of the mountain ranges of the state, from the Sierra Madre and the Medicine Bow on the southeastern end to the Bighorns in the north central part of the state. In Wyoming, the black bear's hold is firm, although each year, more and more summer homes are built in his backyard.

The grizzly, though, stands on a thin ledge. Wyoming's grizzlies seldom get farther from their last, best stronghold,

Yellowstone and Grand Teton national parks. When they do stray farther, they die. In August 2002, an adult male grizzly made the mistake of moseying down into sheep country in the Wyoming Range south of Jackson. That bear was shot after allegedly preying upon domestic sheep. In May 2003, a young male grizzly visited a bait that a hunter had set out to attract a black bear on the Middle Fork of Owl Creek outside Thermopolis. The hunter shot the bear at last light. Only after the bear was dead did he identify it as a grizzly.

When the opportunity to write this book was presented to me, I was hesitant. For as long as I've been able to imagine bears, dream of bears, I've been an advocate for them and for their survival on these last few kernels we are leaving them. The world, I thought, doesn't need another slasher book about bears. But then I read this book's companion volume, *Great Montana Bear Stories* by Ben Long. My thinking changed. Here, I thought, was a chance to tell stories about bears, about how individual bears are, about what amazing animals they are, and—just as importantly—about the people who have come into contact with them. Yes, bears are dangerous, and in this volume there are stories of tragedy and violence, but bears are also incredible. Some are never seen. Some come too close to humans and pay with their lives. Others make our hearts pound with fear. But the bear has much to fear from us as well.

When mountain man Jed Smith was mauled by a grizzly in Wyoming's Black Hills in 1823, the great bear ranged from Mexico to Alaska and from Kansas to California. Today, not even 200 years later, just a fraction of that original range still harbors grizzlies. Most of the best is a small corner of Wyoming.

Shot, poisoned, hunted with hounds, roped and choked to death, trapped . . . the grizzly's history with humans in the last 200 years is no more horrifying than that of any species of wildlife we have endangered. Thankfully, someone cared. We have not gone too far. The bear lives and that is important not only for the bear, but for what he represents.

In the great bear is the tall grass prairie that once swept horizon-wide. In the grizzly are the vast herds of bison, 70,000,000 strong. In the bear live the flocks of lesser prairie chickens that flushed by the thousands in front of the market hunters. We have lost most of these wild things and wild places, but we have not lost this bear.

Keeping the bear is our thin symbol of hope for ourselves. Keeping the grizzly alive and wild is the flicker of promise that humans can be tolerant, can live with natural things, not against them. Our history on this continent has been largely the latter. Our ability to demonstrate the former is our hope.

The bear is a sign. His mere existence is a glimmer of promise for a species—ours—that has a grim history. Our record is not shiny, but there is a corner that yet can be polished and treasured. We haven't been very good at seeing the value in those wild animals that are perceived as threats, real or imagined, to our lives and livelihoods. But the fact that the bear walks the wild Absarokas and lives in the far-back country of Yellowstone and Grand Teton says much about those who came before us, about their vision, about their wisdom in protecting this species that symbolizes the frontier in a world of automobiles and downloadable computer programs. The responsibility now lies upon us to protect enough of the little that is left so the great bear will awe another generation who can craft stories of their own. Wyoming needs bears and so do future Wyomingites.

No finer craftsman, no better conservationist, put it so well as Aldo Leopold in 1949: "There seems to be a tacit assumption that if grizzlies survive in Canada and Alaska, that is good enough. It is not good enough for me."

I'm with Aldo on that one.

Young men with guns

*In the 1800s fur trappers look for trouble with the great
bear, and the bear obliges*

It would be hard to imagine a country more suited for a
person with a wild soul than the West of the early 1800s, and
the sprawled-out land that would become known as Wyoming
was a thrill-seeker's heaven. Those who first tread her soil had
heard but whispers of what lay ahead, tales that sounded at
once fabulous and incredible, yarns of great herds of game, of
Indians, of places where the earth breathed fire. They also heard
about grave dangers, including a giant, ferocious white bear
that roamed the river valleys, open plains, and high mountain
parks. It was an animal that could kill a man with a single blow
from a paw.

The West was adventure, and Wyoming was its heart. To the
north and south, the routes, water holes, and good campsites
were known to an extent, at least along the big river valleys of
the West. The rivers, particularly the Missouri and Yellowstone
to the north and the Arkansas to the south, served as highways,
and beaver fur paid the way. But Wyoming, the dry,
unwelcoming land that lay between these water highways, was
a mystery.

In September 1823, a group of approximately eleven men, a
veritable who's who of mountain men including William
Sublette, Jedediah Smith, Edward Rose, James Clyman, Thomas Fitzpatrick, and Thomas Eddie moved south through the
Black Hills and into northeastern Wyoming. They had been

sent by William Ashley to establish a winter camp and trade with the Crow Indians, thus avoiding more dangerous travel in Blackfeet country to the north. Another goal was finding a way through the Rocky Mountains, and it is likely they had heard of the gentle, sage-blanketed route that would be known as South Pass.

These were young men. Smith, at 24, led the force. Some were even younger, full of adventure, ready to face anything. They may have carried the brand new Hawken Plains rifle, a sleek weapon that would become the mountain man's weapon of choice, but they might also have been carrying old technology in the form of the Kentucky long rifle. By today's standards either weapon was very primitive, shooting one slow ball of lead at a time. Even the Hawken, the best of the era, was pitifully under-powered for big game like grizzly bears.

One day in the Black Hills, the men were leading their horses on foot through a brushy draw when they flushed a grizzly bear from a thick copse of trees. Then, as now, humans got into trouble with grizzly bears when the bears were surprised, hungry, or acting in defense. Usually it was the latter, for dangerous animals and young men with rifles don't mix. This time, though we don't know for sure, the grizzly struck first.

The bear turned and ran into the middle of the pack string, scattering horses and packs left and right. The bear then spun and galloped to the head of the pack train. Smith made for open terrain. He didn't make it.

According to Clyman's journal, the grizzly clamped down on Smith, grabbing him by the head and flinging him to the ground before the mountain men could get into action. The bear mauled him badly, but Smith's ammunition pouch and Bowie knife shielded him from serious internal damage. The bear broke the knife and a couple of Smith's ribs, but the worst of the wounds were on his head. In fact, the bear nearly scalped him. The bear must have either run off or was killed. Clyman's journal focused on the captain's injuries, not what became of the bear.

This was a different breed of man. Though seriously hurt— one of his ears was dangling by a strip of skin—Smith directed his own first aid. Clyman, though he had no experience with such matters, sewed him up.

"I asked the Capt what was best he said [send] one or 2 [men] for water and if you have a needle and thread git it out and sew up my wounds around my head which was bleeding freely I got a pair of scissors and cut off his hair and then began my first Job of d[r]essing wounds upon examination I [found] the bear had taken nearly all of his head in his capcious mouth close to his left eye on one side and clos to his right ear on the other and laid the skull bare to near the crown of the head leaving a white streak whare his teeth passed one of his ears was torn fom his head out to the outer rim after stitching all the other wounds in the best way I was capabl and according to the captains directions the ear being the last I told him I could do nothing for his Eare O you must try to stich up some way or other said he then I put in my needle stiching it through and through and over and over laying the lacerated parts together as nice as I could with my hands water was found in about ame mille when we all moved down and encamped the captain be- ing able to mount his horse and ride to camp whare we pitched a tent the onley one we had and made him as comfortable as circumtances would permit this gave us a lisson on the charcter of the grissly Baare which we did not forget."

Smith lay in camp for a few days, then continued the trek west. The crew made their way to a Crow camp on the Wind River, then plotted a route over South Pass that would become the key to opening Wyoming as a route west. Smith went on to fame as a pathfinder extraordinaire, traveling west to California and Oregon and plotting routes all over the West. He wore his hair long for the rest of his life to cover up the scars. He was killed by a Comanche hunting party in 1831 on the Cimarron River.

It was a shoot-first, ask-questions-later era. Although Smith's mauling was apparently unprovoked, usually travelers of the era went looking for trouble with bears. A decade later, while on an expedition up what would become the Oregon Trail— the route that Smith helped pioneer—John Kirk Townsend had several encounters with grizzly bears.

Townsend, who was part of Nathaniel Wyeth's expedition to the Pacific in 1834, left an excellent chronicle of his adventures, one of the few well-written gems of the era. On June 7 along the Sweetwater River, one of the members of Townsend's party intentionally tangled with a grizzly bear. The man, whom Townsend described as a "greenhorn," had the poor judgment to shoot a bear, and not very well. The bear was only nicked and not happy about it. What's more, the man was mounted on a slow horse.

In Townsend's words: "The bear . . . with a fierce growl of angry malignity, rushed from his cover, and gave chase. . . for the distance of half a mile, the race was hard contested; the bear approaching so near the terrified animal as to snap at his heels, while the equally terrified rider,—who had lost his hat at the start,—used whip and spur with the most frantic diligence, frequently looking behind, from an influence which he could not resist, at his rugged and determined foe, and shrieking in an agony of fear, 'shoot him, shoot him?'"

The man had foolishly fallen about a mile from the main force, and about a dozen men went to his aid. They soon "succeeded in diverting the attention of his pertinacious foe. After he had received the contents of all the guns, he fell, and was soon dispatched. The man rode in among his fellows, pale and

haggard from overwrought feelings, and was probably effectu-
ally cured of a propensity for meddling with grizzly bears."

Townsend himself apparently learned a lesson about grizzly
bears, for a little later in the journey, he showed the good sense
to avoid a conflict with a bear. While hunting geese along a
marsh, Townsend spooked a grizzly. The grizzly rose and
Townsend backed away: "I did not know whether, like a dog, if
the enemy retreated he would not yet give me a chase; so when
I had placed about a hundred yards between us, I wheeled about
and flew, rather than ran, across the plain towards the camp.
Several times during this run for life (as I considered it,) did I
fancy that I heard the bear at my heels; and not daring to look
over my shoulder to ascertain the fact, I only increased my speed,
until the camp was nearly gained, when, from sheer exhaustion
I relaxed my efforts, fell flat upon the ground, and looked behind me. The whole space between me and the copse was un-
tenanted, and I was forced to acknowledge, with a feeling
strongly allied to shame, that my fears alone had represented
the bear in chase of me."

The temptation to mix it up with bears was too much for
many of the young men of the time. Rather than avoid bears,
they went looking for trouble. Warren A. Ferris trapped and
traveled large parts of the West in the 1830s and wrote of his
first encounter with grizzly bears on the North Platte River
near the mouth of the Laramie River. Ferris described the bear
as "a large fierce formidable animal, the most sagacious, most
powerful and most to be feared of all the North American quad-
rupeds."

Ferris wrote an account of his travels in a series of magazine
articles and promised readers "many anecdotes" of grizzly bears
as "the brute and human meet in mutual strife." In particular
Ferris noted how large and how numerous grizzly bears were
in the West. "I have often mistaken them for buffalo, and

discovered my error only when they erected themselves to ascertain what passed near them, which they always do when they hear, see or smell anything unusual." Ferris also tells of a trapper who thought he was stalking buffalo only to find himself in the midst of thirty grizzly bears.

Though perhaps exaggerated, there may be some truth to Ferris's descriptions, particularly about the size of bears. Grizzly bears of the era had a huge protein source in the form of bison and other game, and as with Alaska's coastal brown bears and their salmon diet, it is indeed likely they were large. It is likely, too, that grizzlies gathered in some number to feed at concentrated food sources such as Indian buffalo jumps and other animal slaughter sites, just as they did at the Yellowstone National Park dumps in the 1920s and do today on Alaska's salmon rivers.

But their size was not a deterrent to white boys with guns. In James Marsh's *Four Years in the Rockies,* Isaac Rose, 20, relates a clear case of testosterone poisoning at "Little Jackson Hole" near present day Bondurant, Wyoming, in the late summer of 1835. Rose was camped with several other trappers and some Ute Indians when they noticed a large grizzly bear crossing the meadow near their camp. "Some of the boys thought this a good opportunity to have some sport," Rose recalled, so they decided to take on the bear Indian-style. They borrowed bows from their native friends and mounted to attack. Two trappers rode up on the bear and each shot an arrow into it. But "not being very proficient with this kind of weapon their arrows did not penetrate the body of the bear more than an inch or two."

This, of course, only served to make the bear a little bit upset. The two trappers took turns shooting arrows into the bear. The sport kept up until about fifty arrows were sticking into the bear and not one of them a mortal wound. The tormented bear would charge one trapper until shot by the other, then turn and charge that man. Finally, one of the Utes rode up and put an end to the game by shooting the bear once through the lungs with an arrow.

The area where the men were camped was apparently thick with bears for the very next day some of the men encountered another bear. This time a trapper named Caleb Wilkins, 25, was charged by a bear that came out of a thick patch of chokecherry bushes. Wilkins was mounted on a mule, but the mule couldn't or wouldn't outrun the bear. Instead, the mule relied on the accuracy of its hind feet and unloaded on the bear, "nearly dislocating his jaw."

The bear charged again and the mule kicked again, much to the enjoyment of Wilkins's compadres. "All this time the trappers were laughing and shouting: 'Look out, Caleb!' 'Go it, Caleb' but finding the race was likely to end disastrously for Caleb and the mule, one of the trappers galloped up to the bear and shot him in the shoulder . . ." The other mountain men soon unloaded their weapons into the bear and ended its career as a mule-chaser. This is apparently the incident that gave the bear one of its mountain man nicknames, as several journals written after this event called any grizzly bear "Caleb."

Perhaps the most famous of all trapper journals and certainly the best written is Osborne Russell's *Journal of a Trapper*. Russell traveled all over the West during the mountain man era and he, like other young men, had encounters of his own with the great white bear. In the summer of 1835, Russell was one of a party of seventeen men trapping along the Bear River and one of its tributaries, the Thomas Fork, in extreme western Wyoming.

One day they saw a grizzly bear digging in a marsh near a large stand of willows. The bear, intent on its work, did not hear them coming. "The mulatto approached within 100 yards and shot him through the left shoulder. He gave a hideous growl and sprang into the thicket. The mulatto then said: 'Let him go; he is a dangerous varmint.'"

But Russell, then 21, convinced the man to accompany him into the willows after the wounded bear. Both men slowly took to the bear's trail with rifles cocked and ready. They walked close together, on edge, "when we heard a sullen growl about ten feet from us, which was instantly followed by a spring of the bear toward us, his enormous jaws extended and eyes flashing fire. Oh Heavens! was ever anything so hideous?"

Both men ran. Russell's partner shot and missed and Russell suddenly found himself hemmed in on three sides by an impassable quagmire. "I was obliged to turn about and face him. He came within about ten paces of me, then suddenly stopped and raised his ponderous body erect . . . ." Russell pulled the trigger and luckily shot the bear right through the heart. "He gave one bound from me, uttered a deathly howl and fell dead, but I trembled as if I had an ague fit for half an hour after." Russell then made a vow to "never molest another wounded grizzly bear in a marsh or thicket."

Prior to the white man era, Indians for the most part left grizzly bears alone unless they could attack them with a large force. But when whites set foot in grizzly country, everything changed. The mountain men nearly always attacked. A bear hide could bring four dollars and grizzly claws were a tremendous status symbol. Those bears that survived likely learned that humans posed a new threat. But sometimes, the bear took a toll of its own.

In the summer of 1834, 25-year-old Zenas Leonard was a member of a trapping party that probed the valley of the Smith's Fork of the Bear River in western Wyoming. The force was moving up the drainage when they saw a large grizzly bear lying in the shade at the edge of some woods. Four men, including Leonard, started for the bear to kill it, but the bear heard them and disappeared into the stand of trees. The party split up "intending to surround the bear & chase him out and have some sport," but one of the men foolishly dismounted and followed a "buffaloe path into the brush."

The grizzly was spooked towards the man, and though the man tried to climb a tree, the bear pulled him down by a leg and "tore the tendon of his thigh in the most shocking manner. Before we could get to his aid the bear made off and finally escaped." The party camped there for the night and tried to tend to the wounded man as best they could, but he bled to death.

The famous mountain man and guide Kit Carson was a better tree climber. In the spring of 1834, Carson, then 25, and three other men were trapping the headwaters of the Laramie River near the present-day border of Wyoming and Colorado when Carson decided to go hunting. He found a band of elk and shot one. As soon as he shot, he heard a sound behind him and turned to find two large grizzly bears approaching. "My gun was unloaded and I could not possibly reload it in time to fire. There were some trees at a short distance. I made for them, the bears after me."

Carson threw aside his empty rifle to "make all haste to ascend the tree." He climbed out of reach of the bears and waited for them to leave. One left quickly, but the other bear walked around and around Carson's perch, digging at the base of the young aspens nearby and trying to shake Carson out of the tree. "He finally concluded to leave, of which I was heartily pleased, never having been so scared in my life."

Eventually European fashion changed—silk replaced beaver fur for men's hats—and the era of the mountain man came to an end. Nevertheless, the white bear and the white man had been properly introduced.

"The finest sporting animal on the continent"

Sportsmen from near and far pursue bears as Wyoming's frontier comes to an end

They heard the stories, the stories told around campfires and dining tables, at parties and dances. The West. The West! A few stories went over the water and were told in the homes of earls and lords. The West! The West had been discovered.

By the late 1800s, accounts of adventures in the American West had been printed in books and newspapers. A guidebook had even been published for travelers on the Oregon Trail. No longer was the West the great mystery, the land unknown. Now there were stories, and the stories captured imaginations. Anyone who had just a little ember of adventure smoldering in his or her soul dreamed of one day going.

In our 21st Century eyes, it is hard to imagine the great herds of wildlife that swathed the big country. It's even more difficult to comprehend the killing spree that ensued and harder still to understand the mindset that led to the slaughter. It was multi-cultural—Indians as well as white men did their fair share of unnecessary killing—and multi-generational, spanning almost all of the 1800s. By the late 1870s, the great herds had dwindled considerably, but the stories went on, and sportsmen, especially, yearned for a chance to explore and hunt the wildest regions.

Bison, elk, antelope, big-eared deer, moose, black bear. It was a sporting man's wish list. At the very top of this list sat an amazing creature rumored to be fierce beyond imagination, an animal that took a wagonload of ammunition to bring down, an animal worthy of an adventuring man—the mighty grizzly bear. The place was awash with sporting men. In the 1850s Sir St. George Gore from Ireland took to the West like a tornado, bringing a herd of more than 100 horses, 3 milk cows, 50 hunting dogs, and 40 employees on a killing spree that lasted three years and stretched all across the West. By the time Gore arrived back in civilization after a swing through the country that would become Wyoming, he and his hunters had killed 105 bears, 1,600 elk and deer, and more than 2,000 bison. This kind of carnage left virtually nothing behind other than bones and spoiled meat, no contribution to natural history, and nothing for science.

Then came another Irish aristocrat, the Earl of Dunraven, Windham Thomas Wyndham-Quin. Gore was a friend of Dunraven's family and Gore's tales were recounted to the young Dunraven as he was growing up in Ireland. He, too, yearned for the West, probably as much to get away from his five sisters as anything. So he embarked on an adventure to the great land and left a wonderful account of that trip in *The Great Divide*, published in 1876. The tale covers his adventures getting to Yellowstone National Park and what he found there. It was his second trip West and he had already met such flamboyant and famous characters as William F. "Buffalo Bill" Cody and John "Texas Jack" Omohundro in North Platte, Nebraska, in 1871. On that trip, Dunraven brought down his first elk and his first bull bison. But his expedition to the Yellowstone in 1874 would be his most ambitious. Unlike Gore, Dunraven's expedition was a very modest force. It was comprised of Texas Jack for a scout, a doctor, a cook, a servant, a local rancher named Boteler, and Dunraven's cousin Captain C. Wynne, not to mention Dunraven's collie, Tweed.

Besides taking in the sights of the new park—Yellowstone was now two years old—Dunraven thought he'd sample some of the sporting opportunities open to a man of gusto. One of these was hunting, and near the top of his list was the grizzly bear. (Hunting in the park was legal until 1883, when it was made a sanctuary for all animals, including grizzlies.)

Dunraven wrote of the great bear, "If this list be not suffi- cient, and if it be considered that an element of danger is neces- sary, the sportsman will be glad to hear that nowhere, save per- haps in Southern California, will he be more likely to encoun- ter *Ursus horribilis*, the grizzly bear. If he has ever pursued, or been pursued by that unpleasant beast, he will be gratified to learn that, as a rule, pine-trees are numerous and not difficult to climb.

"It is a fortunate dispensation that the only dangerous vari- ety of the genus in America cannot climb. The black bear, it is true, will ascend any tree that he can clasp with his muscular arms; but he is a thoroughly reasonable animal, and is fully alive to the cogent logic of a bullet; whereas the grizzly is an intractable brute. Happily, however, he is no gymnast; and from the security of a tree-top a man can laugh his adversary to scorn."

Dunraven admits he undertook his adventure solely for adventure's sake and not for science, but he did pen some inter- esting natural history. One day as Dunraven and Boteler were in the lead, they ran across a herd of elk. The two men dropped three cows and then made their camp right there. While they were lounging around the campfire having a smoke, basking in the success of the day and enjoying the cool of a Rocky Moun- tain autumn, a bull elk bugled from behind camp. Dunraven sneaked close to the bull and dropped it as well, taking only the head and the hide back to camp.

That night and the following several nights, the four car- casses were visited by grizzly bears. Sometimes as many as four dined on the elk but frustrated the hunters greatly by slipping back into the forest by dawn. "It was impossible to get a chance at them at night, for there was no moon, and the sky was invariably cloudy and overcast; and during the day, they stowed themselves away among the crags, defying detection. We were very unlucky with them indeed, for though bears were plentiful in the valley, and the members of our party had interviews with them, we only got one, a middling-sized beast weighing about 800 pounds," wrote Dunraven. If an 800-pound grizzly was a "middling-sized beast" to Dunraven, it's hard to imagine what a big bear would have looked like.

While at this camp, Dunraven did get a chance to make some interesting observations in how grizzlies cache food. "I had hung a hind-quarter of one of the does (cows) on a branch, well out of reach, as I supposed, and had left the skin on the ground. To my great astonishment, on going to look for it in the morning, I found the meat had been thrown down by a bear, carried about 300 yards, and deposited under a tree. The brute had then returned, taken the skin, spread it carefully over the flesh, scraped up earth over the edges, patted it all down hard and smooth, and departed without eating a morsel. All the carcasses were treated in the same way, the joints being pulled asunder and buried under heaps of earth, sticks, and stones. The beasts must have worked very hard, for the ground was all torn up and trampled by them, and stank horribly of bear."

The Dunraven party stayed at the camp for several days, never far from the elk carcasses. After several days of eating nothing but elk meat, Texas Jack went looking for a white-tailed deer and some venison. He walked alone in a big circle and ended up back at one of the elk carcasses. There he found a large grizzly bear. He reported his tale back at camp.

"Jack came in quite early, looking rather flustered, sat down, filled his pipe, and said, 'J—s! I have seen the biggest bear in the world. D—n me if he didn't scare me properly. Give me a drink and I'll tell you.'"

The fabled frontiersman then launched into an entertaining natural history observation. "'When I got near where the first elk was killed I saw something moving, and dropped behind a tree. There, within sixty yards of me, was a grizzly as big as all outside. By G—d, he was a tearer, I tell you."

In the 1870s the sight of a wild animal, any wild animal, usually was cause for hurling as much lead as possible its way. Had it not been for the fact that Texas Jack was out of breath and needed to rest before he could take a steady shot, he might not have seen what he did see, which turned out to be an excellent observation of a grizzly caching food.

The plainsman continued: "I'll be dog-goned if ever I saw such a comical devil in my life. He was as lively as a cow's tail in flytime, jumping round the carcass, covering it with mud, and plastering and patting it down with his feet, grumbling to himself all the time, as if he thought it was a burning shame that elk did not cover themselves up when they died. When he had got it all fixed to his satisfaction, he would move off towards the cliff, and immediately two or three whisky-jacks (gray jays), that had been perched on the trees looking on, would drop down on the carcass and begin picking and fluttering about. Before he had gone far the old bear would look round, and, seeing them interfering with his work, would get real mad, and come lumbering back in a hell of a rage, drive off the birds, and pile up some more earth and mud. This sort of game went on for some time. Finally I got a fair broadside shot, and, taking a steady sight, I fired. You should have heard the yell he gave; it made me feel sort of kind of queer, I tell you. I never heard any beast roar like it before, and I hope I never may again; it was the most awful noise you can imagine. He spun round at the shot, sat up on his haunches, tore the earth up, and flung it about,

boxed the trees with his hands, making the bark fly again, looking for what hurt him, and at last, having vented his rage a little
and seeing nothing, turned and skinned out for the rocks, as if
the devil kicked him. No Sir! You bet your life he didn't see me.
I lay on the grass as flat, by G—d as a flap-jack until he was out
of sight. Well, all right; laugh if you like, but wait till you see
one, and then you'll find out how you feel. I don't want to have
any more bear-hunting alone, anyhow. It's all well enough with
the black bears down south; I don't mind them; but I ain't a
going to fool round alone among these grizzlies, I tell you.'"

The bear was killed some days later back at the carcasses, but
Dunraven doesn't mention who killed it. Texas Jack had shot
too low and "the bullet had done no damage."

The Dunraven party had a grand time wandering the park,
hunting mountain sheep and elk, and taking in the sights. The
earl also recorded temperatures from various hot springs and
made dozens of interesting observations about wildlife. *The Great
Divide* was popular reading for many years following its publication and today is still very entertaining. Dunraven Pass and
Dunraven Peak in Yellowstone were named after the talented
earl.

The same year that Dunraven was having the time of his life
in Yellowstone, another colorful character was exploring a distant corner of what would become Wyoming. General George
Armstrong Custer had his chance at a grizzly bear while leading
his famous Black Hills Expedition of 1874. Along on the trip
were a number of very competent people, not the least of whom
were the legendary scout Luther North and the great naturalist
George Bird Grinnell.

One day Grinnell and North were riding together when they
heard a barrage of gunshots over a nearby hill. When they galloped to investigate, they found Custer along with the scout
Bloody Knife, Captain William Ludlow, and an enlisted man

identified only as Private Noonan standing over the carcass of a large, old male grizzly. They were debating who had dealt the fatal bullet. North wryly commented later, "The bear was dead before we reached the spot, so I didn't have a chance to get in a shot and claim that I killed it."

Custer, naturally, ended up with the spoils and he triumphantly wrote his wife, Elizabeth, that he arrived at the very pinnacle of a hunter's life: "I have killed my Grizzley." There are two photographs of Custer and his crew posing triumphantly with the old bear. Custer distributed the meat of the old bear among his troops, but a soldier's diary noted that the meat was like chewing on shoe leather, "Bear meat from a young animal is good, but from an old one is hardly fit to eat."

Custer wasn't the only Army man who enjoyed the sporting life. General George Crook, who was to have met up with Custer before the latter became a carcass on the Little Bighorn in 1876, was a bear hunter himself. In 1889, Crook made a hunting foray into Wyoming, traveling some of the same country where years earlier he had led troops into the battle of the Rosebud a few days before Custer and his soldiers were slaughtered.

Crook roamed his old stomping grounds looking for game and carrying a .40-90 rifle with a scope that ran the entire length of the barrel. Along on the hunt was Webb Hayes, the son of President Rutherford B. Hayes. Hayes pulled duty as the hunt's photographer. The party also included a number of Indian scouts and others. During the expedition, the Crook party downed five grizzlies, five bighorn sheep, one bull elk, and 80 mule deer. The fact that no buffalo were taken and only one elk is testament to the rapid decline of wildlife during this "shoot anything that moves" era.

When it came to pure bear hunting, especially grizzly hunting, no man can match the impact on the Wyoming bear population that Col. William D. Pickett had from 1877 to 1904.

Pickett was one of the first settlers in the Greybull River country near present-day Meeteetse. Later in his career, he was a member of the famed Boone and Crockett Club, which had Theodore Roosevelt as its president and conservation as its mission. Archibald Rogers, one of Pickett's neighbors on the Greybull, served as secretary and treasurer for the club.

Both Rogers and Pickett did some serious damage to the grizzly bear population around Meeteetse during the 1880s and 1890s, probably explaining, in part, why the country was grizzly-free for most of the next century. In 1891 Rogers wrote, "Probably more horrible lies have been told by bear-hunters than any other class of men, except, perhaps, fishermen, who are renowned for their yarns. However, I trust that in the case of the few instances I have to give of my experience I can keep fairly within the bounds of truth."

One of these truths was the fact that his neighbor, Pickett, was a bear slaying son of a gun. Rogers wrote of the colonel that he "has killed more bears than any man I know of . . . ." Grinnell, who was above reproach as a naturalist and sportsman, thought highly enough of Pickett to write that he "has had an experience in hunting the grizzly bear greater probably than that of any man who ever lived." Grinnell wrote those words in the preface to the Boone and Crockett Club's book, *Hunting at High Altitudes*, published in 1913. Most of the book is Pickett's "Memories of a Bear Hunter," in which he chronicles his adventures hunting grizzly bears in Wyoming. The frontispiece of the book is a portrait of the legendary bear hunter himself.

After serving as an engineer in the Army of the Confederacy during the Civil War, Pickett was drawn west like so many veterans. He wanted to hunt bear and in September 1877, he got his chance when he entered Yellowstone National Park in search of grizzlies.

Pickett was determined to hunt before the snow flew. He and Jack Bean, a local man who had an excellent reputation as a scout and a woodsman, left Bozeman, Montana, on September 11. By the 16th the men were deep in the park at the foot of Mt. Washburn, and it was raining. The pair pressed on and the rain turned to snow. Eventually the snow got so deep that Pickett and Bean had to dismount and lead their horses up the mountain. Then they saw a large bear approaching through the blizzard. Pickett waited until the bear was within 100 yards and opened fire. Bean joined the shooting and both men emptied their rifles at the bear. Eventually they brought the grizzly down.

Pickett wrote: "The excitement caused by this incident and my enthusiasm on killing my first grizzly—for I claimed the bear—dispelled at once all feelings of hardship and fatigue. The bear was a grizzly of about four hundred pounds weight, fat and with a fine pelt."

Unfortunately they left that fine pelt to waste and left all of the bear meat except a few steaks. Then they pressed on to a camp. That night they roasted the steaks over a fire. "We made fine beds of pine boughs, but I ate too much bear and did not rest well. That bear was taking post-mortem revenge on each of us," Pickett wrote.

For the next several years, Pickett prowled all over the country from the headwaters of the Shoshone down to the Greybull. He killed so many bears that most only warranted a sentence or two in his memoir. "Bears were fairly abundant, but I secured only two, and without adventure." Or, "That night a bear, believing that in the timber he would be safe, came to feed before dark. In the morning a seat had been arranged on the limb of a nearby pine, and as the bear approached, I easily killed him with a single shot." And, "I killed a large grizzly with a dark, well-furred robe. He required only a single shot and gave no trouble."

But Pickett goes into great detail about the bears that were a little harder to kill. In 1880 he was camped in Yellowstone while trying to search for a pass to the east known as Jones' Pass. "One morning, just before September 30, we had been kept housed in the tent by a cold, drizzling rain, but about 9 o'clock, the rain having ceased, I stepped outside and looked around. Just in front of the tent and about a hundred and fifty yards toward the lake, was a grizzly bear aimlessly rooting in the ground. I stepped into the tent, secured my rifle and cartridge belt and passed out. My dog Nip, judging from my actions that something was going to happen, followed at heel, though I did not notice him. Meantime, the bear had moved to the left and was a little bit further off. I concluded from its careless actions in full view of the tent that it was not much afraid, and rapidly approached it. When within about 125 yards, I dropped on one knee and prepared to fire. In the meantime, it paid no attention to me. When it exposed its side, I fired. As if expecting it, and without looking around, the bear came charging directly toward me, with long jumps. The dog met it about half way, dashed at it, when it turned and again exposed its side. I fired again. At the crack of the rifle the bear left the dog and dashed straight toward me. The dog was unable to stop the charge, but when within twenty feet I delivered another shot, which stopped her, for it proved to be a female."

Pickett's experiences confirmed what many frontiersmen before and after him had experienced: grizzly bears were very seldom the aggressors and often just wanted to be left alone. Noted the great northwestern Wyoming hunting guide and grizzly slayer Ned Frost, "He is a peaceful, shy individual when left alone, but he can become the most savage, raging beast on earth once he is aroused."

The year before he founded his ranch on the Greybull, Pickett took a foray into the country looking for bears. In late summer and early fall 1881, Pickett hammered the local bear population. "During these two months from the camp on the head of Meeteetse Creek and the camp on the Grey Bull and from intermediate camps I killed nineteen grizzlies, the majority of them large, with well furred robes. Four grizzlies had been killed before this, but in two cases the robes were not good and were not saved. Twenty-one hides were taken into winter quarters at Bozeman."

In 1882 Pickett founded his ranch on the Greybull River and was busy killing bears in the mountains around his ranch. One night Pickett killed four bears that had come to feed on cattle that had died during a stampede. Pickett named a nearby creek Four Bear Creek and a post office later carried that name. After 1883 Pickett devoted himself to politics and to building his cattle ranch. He served in the Wyoming Legislature and has been given credit as the founder of Big Horn County.

It's hard to say how many grizzlies Pickett killed during his time in Wyoming and Montana. In his 1900 novel, *Biography of a Grizzly*, the novelist Ernest Thompson Seton made Pickett the evil cattle baron who slaughtered the bear protagonist's mother and siblings. The grizzly bear population on the Greybull River probably breathed a collective sigh of relief in 1904 when Pickett sold his ranch and moved to Kentucky.

In writing of his adventures, Pickett made an interesting observation about a bear's ability to sense danger. Pickett called it "psychological magnetism." He explained, "This is that when from any cause one person is intently thinking of someone in front of him and at the same time gazing at him, the object of his thoughts will involuntarily turn his head and look straight at the gazer. The same psychological fact obtains between man and some of the lower animals."

Then Pickett described how he had shot and wounded a bear that he had stalked while it was feeding on an elk carcass (most of the grizzlies that Pickett shot during his forays as a bear hunter were shot over elk, cattle, or other carcasses as bait). Before Pickett could take his first shot, the bear sensed him and jumped up suddenly and ran off, but Pickett was able to hit it once on the run. He tracked the bear until dark and then lost its trail. He never found the bear again, but he did note, "The discovery by the bear that I was approaching convinced me of the truth of the theory of a psychological magnetism that I have spoken of before. This bear could not possibly have seen me nor taken alarm at any noise that I made, for I was in moccasins and the ground was level and clear of brush. Also I had the wind of him."

During this era another famous grizzly bear hunter shot at least one great grizzly bear in the Big Horn Mountains. Theodore Roosevelt and William Merrifield, one of the cowboys working on Roosevelt's ranch in North Dakota, made a hunting trip into Wyoming's Big Horns in the early 1880s. During that trip, Roosevelt tracked a huge grizzly into the thick timber. The bear had been feeding on the carcass of a black bear that the hunters had taken earlier, as well as the carcass of a bull elk they had shot. Wearing moccasins, Roosevelt walked to within eight yards of the massive animal before it jumped from its daybed. With one shot from his .45-70, the future president of the United States dropped the grizzly in its tracks. The bear had been shot between the eyes and Roosevelt estimated its weight at more than 1,000 pounds. Roosevelt was an expert naturalist and several authorities believe that his guess of that grizzly's weight was dead on.

One more expert naturalist, a bear hunter turned bear conservationist, deserves mention. As a child growing up in the east, William H. Wright admitted his life was most influenced by a little book entitled, *The Adventures of John Capen Adams, Grizzly Bear Hunter of California*. Wright consumed the book, and even got to see a grizzly bear in a circus that was reported to have been captured by Adams. He was enamored. Bears, both black and grizzly, would be the propelling forces for his life's work. In 1909, Wright penned *The Grizzly Bear*, which even today is an excellent work filled with valid and important observations. *The Grizzly Bear* stood as one of the best natural history books on the bear for decades after its publication. Wright wrote another outstanding natural history book, *The Black Bear*, the next year.

After years of shooting grizzlies, mostly in Washington and British Columbia, Wright put down his rifle and turned his attention to studying the grizzlies. Now his tool was a camera, and in 1906 he made a foray to Yellowstone National Park in search of grizzly bears. This was a man who "had some bark on him." Unarmed and at night, Wright set up his camera and flash powder along trails used by grizzlies to the various hotel dumps. He worked hard at getting a picture of a grizzly, and even though these bears were feeding on human foods, Wright found that the big bears were incredibly elusive.

One night Wright set up his camera along a well used bear trail that led to a park where bears had been grazing. He stretched a piece of thread across the trail, hoping that when a bear came along and hit the thread, it would trigger the flash powder and illuminate the bear so Wright could get a picture.

"For some hours I waited in the bushes and fought gnats and mosquitoes. I saw several black bears pass along the hillside, but not a grizzly showed his nose until after the sun had set and the little marsh in the park was covered with a mantle of fog. Suddenly then, far up the trail, appeared what first looked like a shadow, so slowly and silently did it move. But I knew at once, by the motion of the head and the long stride, that a grizzly was coming to the bottom for a few roots and a feed of grass.

"I watched closely to see if he acted differently from bears elsewhere that are supposed to know less of man. I could not, however, detect the slightest difference in his actions from those of bears that had never seen Yellowstone Park. All his movements were furtive and cautious, as if he expected to meet an enemy at every step. He would advance a few feet, and then stop, turn his head from side to side, scent the air, and peer in every direction.

"I was, of course, very anxious to see what he would do when he came to the thread across the trail, and I had not long to wait, for he came on steadily but slowly and, when within ten feet of the thread, he stopped, poked out his nose and sniffed two or three times, raised up on his hind feet, took a few more sniffs, and then bolted up the trail in the direction from which he had come. This bear did not seem to have been very successfully tamed."

Wright kept at it, setting up his primitive camera and its trigger mechanism. A whole series of mishaps befell the naturalist, but he was undaunted. Sometimes the bears would detect the trip thread, sometimes the flash would not go off, and sometimes not enough flash powder was used. All the while, Wright perfected his techniques.

In the summer of 1908, Wright was back, trying to get a good picture of a grizzly bear at night. This time he enlisted the help of a young accomplice, J.B. Kerfoot. Many of the better photographs published in *The Grizzly Bear* were taken by Kerfoot. Wright also rigged up another system where he could pull a string that would set off the flash in his set camera. He spent the better part of the summer stalking bears at night and his recounting of those tales is quite entertaining. One can imagine the old bear hunter, who in the same book told of killing five grizzlies with five shots, trying to get good pictures of live bears instead of skins of dead ones. In the photography of bears, he found perhaps his greatest bear "hunting" challenge.

Once he decided that instead of being stealthy, he would leave his scent all over the area in the hopes of confusing the bear so he could get a good picture. He was still using the trip-wire method and he hoped the grizzlies would be distracted by his scent and hit the wire. The camera was set along a well-used trail and Wright walked back and forth along the trail to leave lots of human scent and then " concealed myself where I could watch without being seen.

"The first bear delegation numbered three . . . I judged them to be nearly three years old, and they would have weighed, I should say, in the neighborhood of three hundred pounds apiece. They were as sleek as seals, and one of them had a beautiful silver coat. When they reached the point to which I had walked up the trail, they stopped and scented for a few moments, turned their heads in the direction in which I had gone, and then came on, paying no further attention to the matter. This encouraged me, and I began to think that my ruse was to prove successful; but when he reached the wire the leader stopped abruptly, and the three then stood up, looked at each other knowingly, and then, for all the world as though they inferred a connection between my scent and the presence of the wire, began methodically to track me up.

"I was standing near a tree, and, not having expected any such move on their part, I had not taken the precaution to step back out of sight, and now I did not dare move for fear of frightening them. I therefore stood absolutely still and watched their play with close attention and absorbed interest. They followed my every turn as unerringly as a hound follows a hare, and came on withal as silently as three shadows. Of course I had been careful to select a station to leeward of the trail, and this now helped to postpone their discovery of me. When within fifty feet of me they came to a fallen log, and, when the leader had his front paws on this, he stopped and looked ahead as though he felt he was nearing that which he sought. The second bear started to pass him, but he turned his head and very gently took his companion by the nose with his mouth, whereupon he also stopped, and they both looked straight at me. However, as I did not move a muscle, they seemed unable to make out whether I was a living object or an inanimate one, and they again moved cautiously forward, still in absolute silence. When about twenty-five feet away, they again stood up and examined me intently, evidently doubting whether I were a bona-fide stump. Here, indeed, would have been a glorious opportunity, had I a camera in hand, and had there been a trifle more light.

"But they had come as far as they cared to. Dropping silently on to all-fours, they suddenly abandoned their investigations and bolted, only to stop at the end of a hundred feet, stand up again, again approach within fifty feet or so of me, and then turn aside and trail away through the trees."

Wright and Kerfoot spent much of the summer of 1908 trying to get a photograph of a particularly large grizzly. "It was not until the last night of all that I got another chance at the big fellow . . . about nine o'clock, my big friend came along. He was just passing a small fir-tree when I pulled the string, and it seemed to me, and I dare say to him, as though the end of the world had come. The flash exploded with a noise like a twelve-inch gun, and a shower of burning particles rose in the air and glowed for more than a second.

"When we developed the plate we found that the old bear had backed up against the tree and, with bared teeth and savage mien, had faced the unexpected danger. The picture was far from perfect, but it gives a notion of his splendid proportions and his savage courage. I have called it 'At Bay.'" Wright, though he shot and killed dozens of grizzlies in his lifetime, seemed prouder of this trophy than of any other.

One other grizzly bear hunter in Wyoming seemed to have been impressed by the great bears so much that he didn't kill as many as he could have. In 1936, the celebrated novelist Ernest Hemingway visited the headwaters of the Clark's Fork of the Yellowstone. He spent the summer working on his novel, *To Have and Have Not*, and that fall, he went hunting. It was his third summer in this remote and rugged part of Wyoming just outside the seldom-visited northeastern corner of Yellowstone.

There had been rumors of grizzly bears near the headwaters of Crandall Creek, and Hemingway's guide and host for that summer, Lawrence Nordquist, shot a couple of mules far up in the drainage to use for bait. Nordquist had been guiding hunters in the region for years from his small dude ranch on the Clark's Fork. Shortly afterwards, Hemingway got his first chance on a Wyoming grizzly. He wrote about it in an essay for *Vogue* magazine.

"You remembered coming on the three grizzlies in the high country at the head of Crandall Creek. You heard a crash of timber and thought it was a cow elk bolting, and then there they were, in broken shadow, running with an easy, lurching smoothness, the afternoon sun making their coats a soft bristling silver."

Hemingway shot the largest of the bears and then another. That second shot was one that he would regret. He wrote his editor, Maxwell Perkins, that "I could have killed the three I think but they were so damned handsome I was sorry I killed more than the one but at the time did not have much time to decide."

That would be Hemingway's last extended stay in the valley. That summer the Beartooth Highway punched into the remote region, an encroachment of civilization that Hemingway deeply lamented. Except for a brief visit in 1939, he would not be back.

Almost all of the great bear hunters of the time were visitors to Wyoming. But maybe the greatest bear hunter of them all was a homegrown product. Ned W. Frost grew up on a ranch in the Cody country and earned his living guiding hunters in the nearby high country. At one point, he claimed to have been in on the demise of more than 350 grizzly bears.

When Frost was a young boy on the family ranch on Sage Creek outside Cody, he killed his first grizzly bear. His father had been losing cattle to grizzlies and had set traps for them. One day he told the young boy to go check the traps, and Ned took his father's .45-90 Winchester. At the trap site, he found and shot a large grizzly. He was only about seven years old.

In 1916 Frost was making his living by taking tourists into the Yellowstone country on wagons. By this time, he had gotten used to losing food to camp-raiding bears, writing, "Many are the hams and slabs of bacon I have donated to the *ursus* family of night prowlers during these years. Many a time have I run them off with clubs or firebrands; while on the contrary, many a time has some old silver-tip bluffed me out by showing that he was there for results and there was nothing for me to do but to stand by and let him help himself."

On the night of August 14, 1916, Frost was camping about four miles east of the Lake Hotel when a grizzly visited his camp. "On this particular night . . . we had noticed some unusually large grizzly tracks around camp. Consequently we had sat up rather later than usual around the camp fire, reassuring Mr. and Mrs. Frothingham of Boston, whom I was guiding on this trip, that there was absolutely no danger; that bears were perfectly harmless if you did not molest them at their prowling and predatory excursions; and that there was not a case on record where a bear had made an unprovoked attack on a human being."

Finally, everyone turned in. Frost, the camp cook, and the wrangler bedded in the open, "one on each side of the pack containing the provisions. It was a clear moonlight night, but rather cool and cheerless, so I put an extra heavy canvas pack cover over my sleeping bag just before I turned in. This I have often thought since may have been the means of saving my life. Shorty, Jonesy and I had been working together for years thru the Yellowstone and the hunting country. We felt no uneasiness whatever as we lay down to rest, and were all sound asleep almost immediately.

"At about half an hour after midnight we were aroused by the most blood-curdling yells that I ever heard come from human kind. Raising myself in my sleeping bag, I saw there in the bright moonlight about fifteen feet away from me a huge grizzly. He had Jonsey by the back and was shaking him, bed and all, as a terrior (sic) shakes a rat. Yelling at the top of my voice, as Shorty was also doing, I threw my pillow. As the white mass landed just in front of him, the bear flung Jonsey to the ground and started back. His fiery little green balls of eyes caught sight of me as I sat up in bed waving my arms over my head in a vain attempt to scare him."

Instead the grizzly lunged for Frost, who ducked down into his bedroll beneath the heavy canvas cover. The bear pulled and tossed the bedroll and started to drag Frost off into the woods inside his bedroll, biting the guide's legs and knees through the heavy canvas tarp.

"That I am alive today I attribute to a lucky fluke. After shaking and carrying me along several times he finally got a mouthful of sleeping bag only and with a vicious shake threw me clear of the bag, like a potato out of a hole in the sack. Head over heels I went for several yards, landing under some low-hanging jack pine branches. I grasped these, intending to climb the tree, but my lacerated knees refused to bear my weight, so I went hand over hand—to the very top, you may be sure, and the wonder is I am not going yet."

The bear ran off after the entire camp came awake. Two doctors and a nurse at the Lake Hotel stitched up Frost and Jonesy. "Jonesy had four places in his back stitched up; and his face was sort of smeared sidewise a bit where old Bruin had stepped on it. I had six wounds in my legs sewed up. In one the main artery, the size of a lead pencil, was exposed for two inches but not ruptured. If it had been I should have bled to death in ten minutes."

Two weeks later, a grizzly killed a teamster named Jack Welch not far from where Frost's attack occurred. Not surprisingly, bear "attractants" were involved; Welch and his companions were sleeping beneath a wagon filled with grain and hay when the attack occurred.

It's amazing how far we have come in bear-proofing techniques. The method for protecting one's food from bears in those days was to sleep right with it. This was an old mountain man's trick, sleeping right next to a fresh kill, even using the carcass as a pillow.

Sleeping right next to the food today is seen as lunacy, but in that era, that's how it was done. Everyone apparently did it because they felt that was the best way to defend the food. Moreover, this was remote country, where the nearest town was miles and miles away by horseback or wagon and the loss of provisions could spell serious trouble. They didn't just hike back to the trailhead and drive to the store for a resupply if a bear got their food.

Frost wrote up the story of his attack in the April 1919 issue of the sporting magazine *Outdoor Life*. For a while, he seemed to resent grizzlies, vowing in that article "a desire to wage war to the death on any member of the family of *ursus horribilis*, from cubhood to old age.

"And only a few weeks ago I had the pleasure of exploding a .280 Ross in an extra big old boy, one dark stormy night (and not in the Yellowstone Park either) who was nosing around my bed within twenty feet. I don't sleep well any more with those old devils spooking around my bunk, and I can fairly smell one if he comes within miles."

Frost was the real deal. He spent his entire life in the mountains around Cody, guiding hunters and tourists and making a living off the land. By 1939, Frost seemed to have mellowed a little bit. He wrote an entertaining chapter called "Hunting the Grizzly Bear" in the Boone and Crockett Club's book, *North American Big Game*. The veteran grizzly hunter's affection for his nemesis exudes from the pages.

"This animal is the grandest and most rugged individual of them all," wrote Frost. "By birthright he is king of the North American animals, and by reason of his unbelievable strength and dominating courage he has maintained his claim to the ruler's throne."

Frost goes on to espouse on the challenges of hunting the grizzly bear, noting that much of the bear's reputation as a fierce beast was exaggerated. "Like other dangerous game animals, all Grizzlies do not charge. In fact, relatively few do. I have been in at the kill of over three hundred and fifty Grizzlies, but I have seen only a scant dozen determined charges. . . Chasing with dogs, and crowding wounded Grizzlies in thick brush has brought forth no charge in many cases."

Frost closes the chapter with this: "The love of the 'Silver Tip' is deep in my heart. He is a clean liver, a worthwhile adversary and the finest sporting animal on the North American continent today. May he always find life and happiness among the high peaks of the Rocky Mountains."

Something had changed. Perhaps it was the general mellow-ness of age, when a hunter looks back over his life and thinks of the things he has done and those he has not. Perhaps the shift was brought on by the changes in wildlife populations that Frost had seen in his lifetime. He had known Buffalo Bill Cody, a man who had killed thousands of buffalo. Frost himself had seen the tail end of the great frontier and had witnessed the demise of the great herds of game, even in the remote moun-tains. By the time Frost wrote his tribute to the grizzly, the bear had been exterminated from many western states including Arizona, Oregon and California—where the grizzly was the cen-terpiece of the state's flag. For a man who enjoyed hunting and wild animals, the era he lived in must have been a deeply de-pressing time.

Perhaps an event in 1920, only four short years after Frost was mauled in Yellowstone National Park, also had some im-pact on his thinking. Frost was part of an incident that would become one of the most controversial grizzly bear stories in the park's entire history: the killing of a number of grizzly bears by the legendary archers Saxton Pope and Arthur Young. As with many stories, the truth is the lesser-known part of the tale.

"A great big outstanding sporting event"

Legendary archers Pope and Young break all the rules in Yellowstone National Park

On December 8, 1919, a letter came across the Washington, D.C., desk of Stephen T. Mather, director of the National Park Service. The letter was a request from Barton W. Evermann, director of the California Academy of Sciences. It was a plea from one man of conservation to another.

The academy had a new museum at Golden Gate Park in San Francisco and Evermann was busy putting together exhibits. But, he explained, they had a problem: the grizzly bear. The California grizzly, which had once fed on whale carcasses along Southern California beaches and had dug for gophers on the talus slopes of the High Sierra, was gone. Sportsmen, vaqueros, and trappers of the Golden State had successfully wiped it off the face of the earth. Unfortunately for Evermann, the bear went extinct before the academy could shoot a few for museum mounts, in the name of science.

Perhaps Mather could help. The men had visited a few weeks earlier when Mather was in San Francisco, and the letter was apparently a follow up to their conversations. You can almost hear Mather tell Evermann on that visit to "put it in writing." So Evermann did.

"Above all things, a group of the California Grizzly, the bear that occupied such a prominent place in early California history, would be the most appropriate species to show," Evermann wrote. "Alas: the California Grizzly bear is extinct; not a single living example of that great bear is now believed to exist any where; and that we can not have such a group will always be a matter for great regret."

But continued Evermann, the next best thing would be a group of grizzly bears from Yellowstone because the grizzly in Wyoming was "very much like the California species." Would Mather be so kind as to permit the academy to send a person to Yellowstone National Park to collect—a.k.a. kill— "an adult male (the biggest we can get), and adult female, and two cubs" in the interest of science? Then Evermann dangled a big carrot: the exhibit would have a background "showing Yellowstone Park scenery" that "would prove a very fine advertisement of the Park."

Mather mulled the idea for a few days and then penned a response. A promoter at heart, Mather recognized an opportunity to get a little publicity for Yellowstone. In a letter dated December 11, 1919, he embraced the idea, noting, "Your proposal to have this group appear with the Yellowstone Park scenery is right in line with the plan that I put up some time ago with the Field Columbian Museum, suggesting a group of national park scenes as a background for habitat groups like the Rocky Mountain goat in Glacier, the elk of Yellowstone, etcetera. My suggestion, however, was not carried out, owing to the lack of funds at the time, and I am very glad to see a similar suggestion coming from you. There is a great interest taken in Yellowstone Park by Californians, and we are having more and more motor trips from there in the summertime."

A few months later Mather dictated another letter to Evermann, saying: "This letter will serve as a permit for you, or another representative of the California Academy of Science to be designated by you, to kill in Yellowstone National Park four grizzly bears, the heads and hides of which are to be used in

preparing an exhibit in the museum of the California Academy
of Sciences." It was a letter that Mather would deeply regret.

The expedition to hunt grizzlies in the national park started
out badly. Although Mather had advised the academy to send
hunters by May 1 to secure hides in the best condition, they
didn't show up until nearly June. Perhaps the urgency of time
had as much to do as anything with the ugly display of sportsmanship that followed. But perhaps not. For at least one of the
hunters, the expedition to Yellowstone was more about the
weapon and the kill than it was about collecting museum pieces.

Dr. Saxton T. Pope, a San Francisco physician and a sup-
porter of the academy, lobbied from the get-go to lead the expedition to Yellowstone at his own expense. Indeed, if one is to
believe Pope—and believing anything Pope was to write about
the events in Yellowstone is a dangerous business unless you
adore fiction—it was his idea in the first place. The reason he
wanted to be in charge was simple: paramount among his life
goals was to take a grizzly bear with a bow and arrow.

In 1920, most people considered the bow a novelty, a child's
toy that was adequate for target practice but certainly not for
hunting. Pope and his sidekick, Arthur Young, had devoted
their lives to proving otherwise, to proving that the bow and
arrow was a formidable weapon for a sporting adventure. The
men had taken a number of big game species, including black
bear, but nothing as formidable as the legendary grizzly. An
expedition to take what Pope considered North America's most
dangerous game would certainly cement the weapon's value
among the hunting populace. Moreover, an article about
the expedition would sell to a sporting magazine and bring
crucial publicity to the men's work as pioneer archers. The
only problem was that Mather, Yellowswtone Park
Superintendent Horace Albright, and Evermann (he claimed
later) thought the hunters were going to use firearms. Pope claimed

that everyone from the very beginning knew that the bow was to be used.

In late May, Pope and Young arrived in the park loaded for bear. They were toting "two bows apiece and a carrying case containing one hundred and forty-four broadheads, the finest assembly of bows and arrows since the battle of Crecy," wrote Pope. Their bows were made of Oregon yew and stood as tall as a grown man. The wood-shafted arrows "were usual three-eighths birch shafts, carefully selected, straight and true. Their heads were tempered steel, as sharp as daggers."

Along on the trip was Pope's brother, G.D. "Gus" Pope, "a hunter of big game with the gun," as well as Gus's friend "Judge Hulbert of Detroit along with us to see the sport and to give dignity to the party." No doubt their wisest decision was hiring Ned Frost as their guide, a man whom Pope called "the most experienced hunter of grizzly bears in America." Armed with a rifle to back up the archers, Frost was instructed to shoot only in the direst of circumstances.

Upon arriving in the park, the party dropped by the park superintendent's headquarters to say hello. The superintendent was none other than Horace Albright, Director Mather's right hand man. Less than a year earlier, Albright had moved with his young family to take charge of the nation's first and most famous national park. The position was something of a reward for Albright's years of service in Washington. He and Mather were more than colleagues; they were conservation visionaries and fast friends. Albright's new baby boy was named Robert Mather Albright.

Albright gave the expedition his blessing and some advice about where to hunt. He also put park rangers at the disposal of the party. The hunters set up headquarters in a cabin.

For a week, Pope and Young followed at Frost's heels as the guide led them up and down Yellowstone's hills in search of

bear. But no bears were found. Pope later claimed in his account of the hunt that the rangers had killed them all off before
the hunters arrived. Finally, after days of tromping the high
country, the men spotted a bear feeding on a far ridge above
timberline. They planned a stalk.

As they got closer, they could tell the bear was a young one
and that its coat was poor. It was definitely not adequate as a
museum exhibit. This didn't seem to matter to Pope. He wanted
to kill a grizzly with an arrow. "He was not a good specimen,
rather a scrawny, long-nosed male adolescent, but a real grizzly
and would do as a starter," wrote Pope.

The men stalked very close to the bear, within thirty yards,
before the young grizzly saw them. "For one second he half
reared and stared. I drew my bow and as the arrow left the
string, he bounded up the hill. The flying shaft just grazed his
shoulder, parting the fur in its course. Quick as a bouncing
rubber ball, he leaped over the ground and as Young's belated
arrow whizzed past him, he disappeared over the hill crest. . . .
Well, we were glad we missed him, because after all, he was not
the one we were looking for."

A few days later, Frost led his hunters to another opportunity, a sow grizzly bear with three adolescents at her side. The
museum wanted a sow with two little cubs of the year, not two-
year-old cubs, but again, the collection of exhibits was second-
ary to the desire to kill a bear. The men pressed on, stalking the
grizzlies where they lay sleeping on a snowfield, using the contours of the land to hide their approach and ever mindful of the
wind direction.

"As we walked rapidly, stepping with utmost caution, I
answered all the questions of my subconscious fears. 'Hit
them? Why, we will soak them in the gizzard; wreck them!'
'Charge? Let them come on and may the best man win!'
'Die? There never was a fairer, brighter, better day to die

on,'" wrote Pope in an article he later penned for a popular outdoor magazine.

The trio of Frost, Pope, and Young made an impressive stalk of the dozing bears, creeping up a ridge where they could look over into the patch of melting, old snow. "There on the snow, not over twenty-five yards off, lay four grizzly bears, just like so many hearth rugs," wrote Pope. "Instantly, I selected the farthest bear for my mark and at a signal of the eye we drew our great bows to their uttermost and loosed two deadly arrows.

"We struck! There was a roar, they rose, but instead of charging us, they rushed together and began such a fight as few men have seen. My bear, pinioned with an arrow in the shoulder, threw himself on his mother, biting her with savage fury. She in turn bit him in the bloody shoulder and snapped my arrow off short. Then all the cubs attacked her. The growls and bellowing were terrible."

Pope and Young shot more arrows into the young bear and his mother. In the middle of this mayhem, the grizzly sow caught sight of the three men. "I glanced up just in time to see the old female's hair rise on the back of her neck," Pope wrote. "She steadied herself in her wild hurtling and looked directly at us with red glaring eyes. She saw us for the first time! Instinctively I knew she would charge, and she did.

"Quick as thought, she bounded toward us. Two great leaps and she was on us. A gun went off in my ear. The bear was literally knocked head over heels, and fell in backward somersaults down the steep snowbank."

From a distance of only eight yards, Frost had shot the charging sow with his rifle before she could attack the archers. Pope and Young each shot another arrow into her and she died. The three yearlings ran off, although one was mortally wounded and found dead less than a quarter mile away.

The female, though large, "was in poor condition and her pelt was not suitable for museum purposes," wrote Pope. What's more, the cub "was at the high school age and hardly cute enough to be admired."

Upon returning from the hunt, Pope sent word to the museum of their success. The museum telegraphed back that "this size cub was not wanted and that we must secure little ones." Pope tried to cover up the men's inability to take the correct bears with: "It is a hard thing to pick grizzlies to order. You can't go up and inspect them ahead of time."

In truth, these experienced men could tell that the cubs were the wrong size from a long distance, and it's likely they could tell the sub-adult was not the biggest boar grizzly in the hills. They had glassed the bears with binoculars and had successfully stalked close to them over more than a mile of wide-open country. They knew. They just wanted to kill grizzlies with a bow.

Relations between the museum, hunters, and park service deteriorated rapidly after this event. One of the reasons was public relations. Pope and Young wanted publicity about their prowess with archery equipment; the park service didn't want word to get out that they were permitting the killing of several bears from a protected population.

Somehow, whether Pope himself leaked the story or a sleuthing reporter caught wind of the expedition, the *Livingston* (Montana) *Enterprise* ran a story of the hunt. The story stung: "A high-powered rifle in the hands of Guide Jack (sic) Frost saved the bow and arrow hunters of San Francisco from a mauling by a mother grizzly, according to reports from the Yellowstone park.

"The scientists were not content to tackle a mere grizzly, they began their hunting operations on a mother and a cub. The cub was shot by one of the archers and then the movie man missed a treat. There following a few minutes of uncertainty in the world of science as the arrows failed to stop the onrushing mass of fur and muscle. Then Jack Frost's gun barked and barked again and the big missle (sic) stopped Mr. Bear."

This was not the kind of news the park service wanted. Albright sent a note to Washington on June 17, 1920: "I am very sorry about Dr. Pope's bear killing publicity; I do not believe he is responsible for it but it is going to be very embarrassing, and I am having a ranger look him up in the park today for the purpose of having him call me on the telephone. I am going to tell him that he must stop sending telegrams about his hunting and must keep entirely away from the roads and trails of the park or I shall have to recommend that his permit be cancelled. Already some tourists in the park have advised me that they understood we were attempting to completely annihilate the park grizzlies."

Meanwhile, Gus Pope killed a sow grizzly with his rifle. Saxton Pope claimed his brother shot the bear when she charged the archers while they were attempting to kill one of her cubs, but in his story of the expedition, Saxton admits that his brother and the judge hunted grizzlies on their own. So far the party had killed three bears and none of them were exactly what the museum wanted.

Burned by the local press, Albright told Pope and Young that they could take only one more bear. He gave suggestions as to where a big male grizzly might be found. Albright also wrote Mather to recommend that "under no circumstances shall the National Park Service grant another permit for killing animals in this park for museum purposes. In my mind it is exceedingly dangerous policy, and is bound to bring criticism upon the Bureau." In fact, Mather already had been getting letters about the bear hunt from angry tourists, and both men were on edge. Then things got really ugly.

The party had felled three bears, but only one, the young cub, was shot solely with bow and arrow. From the perspective of hunters wanting to prove the capabilities of their favorite weapon, they had accomplished little. Perhaps this failure was motivation enough for the absolute lack of fair chase that followed.

As June dragged on, the party disintegrated. Gus Pope and the judge returned to Detroit, and Frost had business back home in Cody. When he left, Frost left his .35 caliber rifle with the men.

Pope and Young were on their own to collect the fourth and final bear. Without Frost, they were at a loss to find a bear in the wild. But they could find bears at the garbage dump behind the Canyon Hotel, where bears thrilled tourists at evening "bear shows." One of these bears was a nice, big, male grizzly.

Pope and Young asked Albright for permission to shoot the big male behind the hotel. Albright refused "on the ground that I felt that this would spoil the amusement the tourists were then taking in seeing these bears."

There was talk of another large grizzly far up in the Lamar Valley on Miller Creek. Albright wrote, "Becoming discouraged, Doctor Pope telephoned that he could not stay much longer, but would like to kill a big male grizzly known to inhabit the northeast corner of the park. I gave permission for the killing of this bear, and even went to the trouble of having Park Ranger (Henry) Anderson come down to the Buffalo Farm and meet me for the purpose of discussing ways and means of getting the bear."

Pope stopped by the Canyon ranger station where he was given instructions to meet Anderson. "Upon being told that he could not kill bears back of the Canyon Hotel, (Pope) stated that he was on his way to Soda Butte Ranger Station to obtain the big Miller Creek grizzly, going by way of Dunraven Pass.

This word Park Ranger (Clarence) Scoyen, in charge of the Canyon Station, telephoned to me personally," wrote Albright in his official report on the incidents that were to follow.

Instead, the archers faked out the park service. With the superintendent thinking that Pope and Young were in wild Miller Creek, the intrepid archers were in fact right where Albright told them they couldn't be—behind the Canyon Hotel. The men had taken off from Canyon in the direction of the Lamar Valley, but when they got out of sight, they juked. Instead of going to meet ranger Anderson at Soda Butte, "the hunters went out on the road a little ways in the direction of Mount Washburn and then turned back into the timber, where they left their truck," reported Albright. The men hid in an old cabin on a well-worn bear trail that led to the dump, and from there they stuck arrows into not one, but four more bears. Their take included another two-year old bear, a cub of the year, another sow, and a big boar.

That Pope and Young were fantastic archers, expert marksmen, is of no question. These guys could shoot. That Pope and Young, particularly Pope, were sportsmen driven by a high respect for their quarry, governed by the wildlife laws of the time and guided by the ethic of the true hunter and woodsman, is another matter. In Yellowstone, Pope and Young had essentially become poachers, killing three more bears than their permit allowed and hunting in a closed area.

The deception continued. "Evidently these hunters camped back of the hotel for several days while we thought they were hunting in the Soda Butte country, and as the Soda Butte telephone line was down, we could not communicate with that ranger station," wrote Albright.

Then Pope and Young scurried from the park, but not before rangers from Canyon caught them and confiscated all of their bear hides. Albright didn't learn of the poaching until after the

Californians had left the park and had penned a letter from West Yellowstone, Montana, requesting permission to kill yet another bear, a cub. Then the men boarded a train to San Francisco.

Albright was not happy. In his monthly report for July 1920, he wrote: "The publicity given to this work by members of the party has proven most embarrassing to this office and to the Service, and has caused much unfavorable comment.

"After this killing, no bears, either black or grizzly, appeared for nearly ten days, thus causing disappointment to thousands of tourists. Not only were seven bears killed, but four young cubs were left motherless and one other was believed to have been wounded."

Back in California, Pope was telling anyone who would listen about his feats as a bear hunter. He gave a talk to the academy and he put the finishing touches on a lengthy article for a sporting magazine that would later be transformed into a chapter in his book, *Hunting with the Bow and Arrow*.

What's more, even after this over-stepping, Evermann reiterated Pope's request to kill yet another bear cub. Albright responded to this request with, "In view of the fact that seven have already been killed, I am extremely doubtful whether you will be given permission to secure another specimen."

The superintendent goes on to worry about negative press. "Director Mather, I understand, feels particularly badly about the criticism that has been leveled at the Department for permitting the killing—perhaps he has already spoken to you about it. At any rate, I hope something can be done to explain the situation to the general public. It may seem, upon reflection, however, that the least there is said about the expedition the better, and that the best course is to let the whole matter drop. One thing I am sure of, however, and that is that the bows and arrows ought not be mentioned in any other statements about the expedition. We are particularly anxious that no general statement of the final results of Doctor Pope's hunt should be given to the press, as were the circumstances of the killing of the first two or three bears."

Therein lay the essential problem. Pope wanted publicity and was busy scribbling away for a sporting magazine, while Albright was doing everything in his power to "let the whole matter drop." The situation simmered through the summer with Albright and Mather weathering criticism of the park service while Pope and Evermann tried to secure the hides and even get permission to kill one more cub.

At one point, Pope wrote a terse letter to Albright that reads more like the scolding of a naughty boy than a letter to the superintendent of the nation's first and finest national park:

"My dear Mr. Albright: I regret that our expedition has caused you any worry. But when you spoke of adverse criticism of our encounter with the bears, I rather expected that it came from longhaired men or shorthaired women . . . We promise never to do it again. Forgive us and forget. I will send a quieting note to the Academy. All we want now is the hides. Ask Scoyen if he sent them. Very gratefully yours, Saxton Pope."

Four of the bear hides were sent to California, but Mather and company refused to send the other three. Mather, in fact, wrote that "I think we are entirely too mild with these people."

In late August, Pope sent a letter to Mather asking for an official pardon and explaining the circumstances of the hunt. He claimed that his brother Gus had shot the sow grizzly in self-defense. Then he goes on to twist his story of the infamous shooting behind the Canyon Hotel into a harrowing tale set near Dunraven Pass, several miles away from civilization. Pope claimed he and Young constructed a blind near a well-worn bear trail, and from this blind killed an adolescent bear and then several nights later saw another female with cubs of the year.

"This was the type of bear wanted by Dr. Evermann, and we felt that in spite of the fact that we had four specimens, to make our expedition successful we must secure the type of animal wanted by the Museum. Therefore, we shot and killed one of these little cubs," explained Pope.

The mother bear charged. "This was at midnight, but by the light of the moon we saw her coming and I shot and killed her with an arrow in the heart at a distance of less than forty yards."

Pope claimed that a huge male grizzly happened to appear at that very moment, and since the boar was "just the type of bear suitable for the large specimen of the group, and he made demonstrations of an alarming character," Young stuck an arrow into him as well. "Not only were we endangered, but he was a very desirable specimen. My companion and I both shot at him at a distance of sixty yeards (sic), and Mr. Arthur Young shot an arrow completely through his body and ultimately killed him. We trailed him the next morning and found him dead at no great distance from our blind."

Pope goes on to note that the men took great care "to avoid cruelty in our methods of attacking and we tried to observe the spirit of conservation. We were thrown upon our own resources to a great extent, and even though we tried to communicate with Mr. Albright by telephone, we were unable to do so owing to the condition of interrupted telephone service."

Then Pope asks for forgiveness. "We felt, however, that some latitude would be granted us, owing to the exigencies of the occasion and believed that the success of the trip in securing suitable specimens for the Museum would warrant any deviation from the strict letter of our permit....I feel sure that you can give your official pardon to our excess of Zeal, believing that we did it in the interest of science and with no other motive."

Saxton Pope wasn't the only one making a pitch to the park service for forgiveness. Brother Gus got one of his hunting buddies, U.S. Senator Harry S. New of Indiana, involved. The senator wrote Mather, "It occurs to me that this trip of theirs was a great big outstanding sporting event with which we can all afford to be pretty liberal and I hope conditions are such that you can overlook the apparent excess of specimens killed for the outer consideration of the character of this trip and the men engaged in it."

It's probable that Pope didn't know of the bond between Mather and his right hand man, Albright. Yellowstone's superintendent had a different version of the incidents and Mather took that version as the truth. In a terse reply to Pope, Mather requested a meeting in San Francisco in October. Perhaps the good doctor might have talked the director into ordering the release of the remaining hides and forgiving the "excess of Zeal." But any shred of trust between the two sides went completely out the window when Pope's masterpiece hit the streets that very month.

Published in the popular sporting magazine *Forest and Stream, Rod and Gun*, the article was largely fictional and contrary to park wishes, beginning with the very title: "Hunting Grizzly With The Bow. That the age-old implement of the chase still holds its place among modern weapons is conclusively proved by two California sportsmen." Pope not only ignored requests not to mention the type of weapon, he shunned Albright's request to not name the park.

Pope claimed the men were hunting near Dunraven Pass: "We built a blind on the up-hill side of a steep bear trail, some forty yards off. . . Here we proposed to stand our ground." The story regaled the reader with the killing of an adolescent bear and then several nights later, a cub of the year, a sow, and the big boar all in the same moonlit night.

It all started with the approach of a sow with three cubs.

"This night she came; dim shadows, soft velvet foot-falls, and there she was family and all. I whispered to Young, 'Get the cubs.' We waited till they were 40 yards off, then drove the arrows at them. There was a squeal, a jumble of dark figures, a roar from the mother, and they all came tumbling toward us.

"Just then the big fellow appeared on the scene. We had five bears in sight. Turning her head from side to side, trying to find her point of danger, half suspecting the big bear, our dame came toward us. I whispered to Young, 'Shoot the big fellow.' At the same time I drew to the head and drove an arrow at the oncoming female . . . . She was dead in less than twenty seconds."

Then the men let loose at a distance of about sixty yards at the male, but thought they had missed. But upon investigation they found that Young had connected with one of his arrows. The next day, they tracked a blood trail to the big male and found him quite dead.

"One arrow killed him. He was tremendous. His great wide head, his worn and glistening teeth, his massive arms, his vast, ponderous feet and long curved claws,—all were there. He was a wonderful beast. It seemed incredible. I thumped Young on the scapula. 'My boy! I congratulate you!'"

Pope closed his article with several gems, revealing, among other things, that math wasn't his best subject: "At last another day came. We gathered our trophies together and staggered somehow to a trail; packed our camp stuff, hired a machine to get us out of Yellowstone, and sallied forth dripping with salt brine and bear grease, dead for sleep. We were weary almost to intoxication, but the possessors of the two finest bears in Wyoming.

"We left our hides with a ranger to flesh and re-salt, and so the day ended.

"Now, as I write this on the train speeding back to California, it all seems very tame and sweet, but as the cigarette ads say: 'It satisfies.'

"As for the gun, we forgot all about it, until the time we shipped it back to Frost. Not a shot fired!

"The California Academy of Sciences will have a handsome representative group of *Ursus horribilis imperator*. We have the extremely gratifying feeling that we have killed five of the finest grizzly bear in Wyoming,—killed them fair and clean with the bow and arrow."

Mather's private reaction to this saga must have been priceless. Arno Cammerer, who served as acting director of the National Park Service when Mather was traveling, cabled Mather in San Francisco: "Do not fail see article in Forest and Stream for October by Dr. Saxton Pope . . . This is publicity of the most pernicious kind and California Academy of Science deserves greatest censure."

Mather cabled back: "Long interview with Evermann yesterday . . . Declined to give him any more skins. Pope was to speak before Academy last night on hunt. Evermann apparently only interested in securing material for group and not in ethical questions involved."

Even as late as 1924, the museum was still asking the park for permission to kill more bears, but now they wanted a two-year old and a cub. Mather penned a letter in May 1924 that brought the whole matter to a close: "I can readily appreciate the desirability of finishing the bear group; on the other hand I am quite unwilling to do this at the expense of our park animals, already too few in number . . . In the beginning I was somewhat reluctant to giving permission to obtain the grizzlies from Yellowstone, and I even feel more strongly about it now in view of what I consider an unnecessary killing of more bears than were authorized.

"Although for a good cause, in view of all circumstances I feel that my previous action was possibly a mistake, and I therefore am unable to bring myself to believe that I would be justified in granting your request for additional animals." There ended the museum's quest for just the right group of grizzlies to represent their extinct California subspecies.

The academy tried to put as much distance as possible between the doctor and the museum. Albright summed it up this way in a 1921 letter to his boss: "Dr. Evermann blames Dr. Saxton Pope for the trouble with us, and says he is sorry he let Dr. Pope hunt the bears. Dr. Pope, on the other hand, accuses Dr. Evermann of being responsible for all the unfavorable publicity, and says he exceeded the limit of bears prescribed in the permit because he had to kill in order to protect his life. Personally, I think Dr. Pope is the one who is chiefly responsible for the whole fiasco, despite the fact that he is a fine man personally . . . ."

Pope seems to have been coated with a non-stick surface, demonstrating no remorse whatever on his digressions in ethics and fair chase. His book, with a fleshed-out version of the events of 1920, was published in 1925. It, as well as Pope and Young's tireless efforts to prove the effectiveness of the bow and arrow, led to both men being recognized as pioneer archers. Even today, a non-profit club carries the men's names, and archers can enter trophy big game animals into a record book named "Pope and Young."

But this dim incident clouds both men's reputations and Pope leaves us with the impression that he was interested only in the glory of killing bears with a primitive weapon, sportsmanship be damned. Nowhere is this contemptuous attitude more prevalent than in one final anecdote.

On October 20, 1920, Dr. Charles C. Adams, a well-respected naturalist and educator of the time, wrote a brief letter to Evermann about Pope's account in *Forest and Stream*. "I cannot refrain from expressing my great disappointment that the Academy had any part in this really disgraceful affair," Adams wrote. "Had your agent gone there and a Park Ranger killed certain disagreeable specimens for your exhibits, I would not view it so seriously, but doing it as it was, and to cap the climax, advertise it broadcast over the country among sportsmen who have not yet been educated up to a high standard in the preservation of wild life in our National Parks, is a great misfortune.

"I thoroughly believe in scientific work being done on wild life in our Parks, but such a precedent as this will do more, I fear, to retard the advancement of science than any group exhibit that can be made for the Academy."

Evermann wrote back, saying that he couldn't understand the basis for Adams' objections, but noting, "I confess that I do not like Dr. Pope's *Forest and Stream* article very well; but he is an anthropologist and enthusiast with bow and arrow and feels a pride in having demonstrated that the white man can hunt successfully with the Indian's own weapon."

Evermann forwarded this letter on to Pope, and the doctor blasted Adams on, among other things, the scientist's manhood: "That any one can hear of our exploit and not thrill with the hunter's joy seems incredible, and yet it is true. That which to the man of normal emotions brings a throbbing pulse and glistening eye, may cause a painful revulsion to the sensitive soul of the zoophilist.

"What you think is righteous indignation, and count as a virtue, probably has its origin in subnormal endocrin (sic) secretion . . . It is typical of the human female, subjected to frustrated procreative impulses that she develops a fanatical love of animals. Men who have either deficient internal secretion, through inheritance, or who are morbidly repressed or subject to the incidence of senile involution, evidence their abnormality by pathologic emotional responses in these matters. . . .

"That I told our grizzly story in the vernacular of the sportsman, and not in cold academic phrases, may be excused by the fact that it was written for men, printed in a man's magazine and dwelt upon the details that a man wants to know. This story will live, and thrill, when all your monographs crumble on the dusty, forgotten shelves of time."

Of meat and hungry bears

Life-saving lessons for hunters and campers in grizzly country

Here's a sure-fire recipe for a close, possibly deadly, encounter with a grizzly: Go hunting...for trouble. Do everything wrong. Make as little noise as possible. Sneak through the deep woods at all hours of the day. Be quiet. Or, worse yet, make sounds like grizzly food—bugle like a bull elk or blow on a cow call to sound like an elk calf or its mother. Carry a rifle that you can shoot pretty effectively at long range but is not built for shooting something closing rapidly at close range. Or carry an even poorer weapon for such matters, a bow. If you are a good hunter, you'll kill an elk and then your hands and clothes will smell of blood and meat. If you take an elk late in the day, there's a good chance you'll have to leave it overnight and return in the morning to pack it off the mountain. When you do get it off the mountain, you'll likely take the meat to where you are sleeping.

Each year, several thousand hunters do just these things in Wyoming's grizzly bear country. It's almost as if they are trolling for bear, trying to attract a grizzly.

There is no other way. Spend enough time hunting elk in grizzly country, and eventually you'll run into a bear. If you are a successful hunter—if you take that bull or cow elk—your odds of seeing a grizzly increase all the more.

For most nonresident hunters coming to northwestern Wyoming, it's the trip of a lifetime. They save for this trip for years, dreaming of the day they can hunt in country that Theodore Roosevelt and Ernest Hemingway hunted and wrote about. Most are after elk, and they hire an outfitter to supply all of the tools of a deluxe wilderness elk hunt: tents, horses, camping gear, food. Wyoming law requires that nonresident hunters in designated wilderness hire guides, and because of this, outfitters like Nate Vance—until recently the owner of Teton Wilderness Outfitting—can make a living. For twenty-three years, Teton Wilderness Outfitting has guided hundreds of successful hunters.

Outfitting starts in the middle of August, two weeks before the archery hunters arrive. Setting up a big hunting camp in the middle of remote country is a huge undertaking. Vance runs between thirty five and fifty head of horses, loading pack horses and mules with tents and cook stoves and all of the gear needed to make hunters comfortable in a wild setting. Then they head out, heading east into some of the last, best country in the world, up and over treacherous Deer Creek Pass and down into the Thorofare River country.

It's game country: elk, moose, bighorn sheep, mule deer, black bear and grizzly. It's also the most remote hunting camp in the Lower Forty Eight. At a camp just outside the southeastern corner of Yellowstone National Park, Vance, three or four guides, a wrangler and a cook will make their home for two and a half months. From this base, hunters and guides will head onto the Bridger-Teton National Forest searching for that elk of a lifetime, and sometimes finding more.

Hunting in grizzly bear country is harder work than hunting where grizzlies aren't. By law, game carcasses, horse feed, and human food need to be out of reach of a grizzly, either in bear-proof panniers or hung high out-of-reach between trees. Some outfitters even build caches—big platforms not unlike a child's tree fort. Most people abide by federal and state grizzly bear rules because the regulations make sense and because no one in their right mind wants to have 400 or 500 pounds of hungry bear in their camp or on their elk.

In his camps and on his hunts, Vance takes those rules a little farther still, but early one September morning during the 1994 archery season, Vance went against his own rules. In the Vance camp, the cook keeps all the food in bear panniers, which are high-tech boxes approved by the Interagency Grizzly Bear Committee. The panniers are slung on either side of a packhorse. Usually made out of aluminum and quite durable, they can be opened by humans by turning a knob or screw but bears usually can't open them. It's that opposable thumb thing. In Vance's camp, the panniers are stashed in a hole in the ground called the "bear hole" and covered by a very heavy metal plate. This keeps the food cold and out of reach of bears. Usually.

"I'm always the first one up in camp and generally get up about 2:30 in the morning," said Vance. "I was the only one up that morning and I got the fires going in the kitchen and in the cook tent and had the coffee done and heard a noise outside. The morning before, I'd heard the same noise and when I went out the gal that I had just hired as a camp cook was trying to lift the lid off. She had tried to do that herself without me getting her up and I kinda gave her a little scolding and told her I didn't want her lifting that heavy lid so she wouldn't hurt her back.

"Well the morning this happened, I heard a similar noise and without holding to my own rules, walked out without a light in my hand," said Vance, whose rules for hunters and employees includes carrying a flashlight at all times when it's dark outside. "I just stepped out the back of the kitchen thinking it was Chris again. I didn't see a flashlight (coming from the bear hole) and so immediately I knew I was in trouble. I just came right up on a big bear that was five feet from me. I just startled him and he just reacted like bears should react and it was my own fault."

In an instant, the bear was on him. "I heard a woof and smelt that awful breath and whap," said Vance. "There's nothing like the smell of their breath when their face is right there in your face. It's pretty rank."

The bear swatted him and he fell down. The bear "got my head in his mouth and chomped down a time or two and then he picked me up (by the head) and kind of slung me around and I think about then is about when I passed out," said Vance. "I think because he twisted my neck or something and then he bit me in several spots."

Then the bear left and Vance lay behind the cook tent, bleeding. " I don't know how long I laid there," he said. Eventually he came around, got to his feet, and woke up some people in camp. Fortunately one of his longtime clients in camp was a plastic surgeon. The doctor had a full medical kit, including some painkillers, and they set up an impromptu backcountry hospital.

"He stretched me out on the kitchen table and went to sewing and got me put back together," said Vance. The bear had lacerated his scalp and there were bites in Vance's arms, back, and legs, but the injuries weren't severe enough for the outfitter to want to leave the backcountry. In fact, the next day Vance took a client out hunting and the hunter killed an elk.

"The whole thing was my own fault," said Vance. "You know if I'd been adhering to the rules that I ask everybody in camp to go by, I wouldn't have gotten mauled. It was another example of how you just can't be too careful. He wasn't a problem bear, he had never gotten anything around camp so he quit coming around. You know if I'd of even hollered as I walked out the back of the tent, he would have probably took off. I just stepped out to tell Chris to stop lifting on that, that I'd get it, and it wasn't Chris."

The wounds from that encounter have long since healed and the scars are hardly visible today. Although Vance sold his outfitting business a few years ago, he still guides clients for the new owners and still spends months every year in grizzly country.

Wyoming's grizzly bear country hugs the perimeter of Yellowstone National Park, stretching for miles south and east in several massive wilderness areas. Grizzlies in recent years have expanded south into the Wind River Range, and in 2002, a grizzly was confirmed in the Wyoming Range well south of Jackson. But the heart of grizzly country outside the park are the Absaroka Mountains, which are essentially two ranges— the northern and the southern—of timber, wild rivers, tall tough country. It's the kind of country that the forefather of the American idea of wilderness, Aldo Leopold, spoke of when he defined wilderness as "a continuous stretch of country preserved in its natural state, open to lawful hunting and fishing, big enough to absorb a two weeks' pack trip, and kept devoid of roads, artificial trails, cottages, and other works of man." Hunting safely here takes nerve and it takes an ethic of clean, cautious camping.

Some elk hunters think the big bears add to the hunt, giving them an edge, a feeling that they miss in tamer country. Out here, they aren't necessarily atop the food chain and that reality heightens the senses. It not only makes them more cautious and more aware, but better hunters as a result. Other hunters resent grizzlies, feeling the bears are dinosaurs in a fur coat, relics of another time, no good, better dead.

Vance takes it in stride, despite the fact that elk hunting in grizzly country makes him and his guides feel doubly responsible for their clients and makes them work far harder than they

would in country cleansed of grizz. "They are part of the ecosystem and you've got to exist with them," said Vance.

The education for Vance's hunters starts early. As soon as he
learns that the hunters have drawn a coveted elk license from
the Wyoming Game and Fish Department, he sends them pack-
ets of information on hunting in grizzly country. The department itself puts out an information packet that Vance highly
recommends. He also takes it to another level, particularly when
they have an elk down.

"One thing that really helps if you harvest an elk is if you can
bring it in that night and get it up in the meat cache," Vance
said, "because every time you leave a carcass (out overnight)
you are setting yourself up for a future encounter when you go
back to retrieve your elk the next morning."

The elk is cut into quarters and put on pack animals and
moved quickly. Vance even carries roll-up panniers that can be
carried behind the cantle of a riding saddle and used to move
the meat. "Even if we just move the quarters a good half mile
from the harvest site and try to hang them up in a tree and go
back the next day and get them, that helps," said Vance. "Quite
often you can use your saddle horses and just walk all the way
back to camp, and then if we're going into an area where we are
pretty sure we are going to harvest an elk, we take a couple of
pack animals with us. But you can't always do that, it's a good
theory but that's not how it works out all the time.

"But another thing that works really well is to just put ammonia out, you know, pour that out around where you've har-
vested your elk and that will keep bears away for a few days."
Vance carries a quart of ammonia in his saddlebags for just that
purpose, and he pours it around the carcass to keep the bears
away. It's a trick he learned from an Alaska moose-hunting guide.

Vance's bear-avoidance technique leans heavily on common
sense. "If I've seen a lot of bear sign in the area, you know I

kinda move on, and if there's some real frequent sign, I kinda back off of the calling and try to go where there's some elk where there hasn't been a bear in the last twelve to eighteen hours."

Nor do Vance and his guides hunt elk in the middle of the day, when bears are typically bedded down in thick timber. "We back off of the elk hunting in the middle of the day anyway just because so much of our country burned in the fires of '88, so we don't dare pressure those elk all day long," said Vance. "And then we try to avoid evening harvest, leaving the animal out, because if they do come in and get on the carcass, then we've got an encounter the next day when we go retrieve our elk, we just set ourselves up for an encounter."

In camp, this clean-living ethic is practiced in a number of ways. "When the hunters come into camp we go over with them that we don't want them taking anything sweet smelling or any food or anything like that to their tent, and if they have any candy or snacks or things like that, they give it to the cook and she keeps it all in bear proof panniers," said Vance. "Everything that is human food is put in bear proof panniers." Horse feed is put up in a cache out of reach.

The cook takes extra precautions as well, straining all of the dishwater and burning what strains out. She also puts bleach in the dishwater that she throws out and pours bleach around the area where she dumps the dishwater.

"But the main thing is just to not have any food scraps when you pitch out your water, and our cook is very careful that she scrapes everything before she washes it," said Vance.

If a bear should come into camp, the hunters are instructed to stay in their tents so Vance and his crew know where they are and don't have to worry about them.

Camping in grizzly country certainly takes special precautions, but it is when a hunter has taken an elk that the odds of grizzly encounters increase dramatically. It's not some tiny scrap of hash browns attracting a bear but 400 or 500 pounds of meat combined with other smells of a fresh kill—entrails and blood. Fall in the Wyoming high country may mean the hunt of a lifetime for a person, but it also means an important food source for bears—both black and grizzly.

Indeed, grizzlies have come to depend on finding elk meat in the woods each autumn. Mark Haroldson, a biologist with the U.S. Geological Survey and a member of the Interagency Grizzly Bear Committee, recently found a direct correlation between grizzly movement and hunting seasons around Yellowstone National Park. Using radio telemetry records from nineteen radio-collared bears in Yellowstone, Haroldson found that the bears gather at the park border just before hunting season, then move out of the park as hunting begins. Hunters essentially create what biologists call an "eco-center" that attracts grizzlies with an important food source. "It's a lot like a salmon stream," said Haroldson. "In a lot of country there aren't any bears during other times of the year, but once the hunt starts, they move out of the protected area (of Yellowstone National Park) and into the hunt areas. The bears know where and when to go out of the park."

It's little wonder. Each year in the hunting areas around Yellowstone (most of which are in Wyoming), hunters leave behind an estimated 500 tons of bear food in the form of gut piles and other parts that are inedible for humans but delectable for bears. Most of this meat—some 370 tons—is elk.

Haroldson calls the annual infusion of grizzly sustenance a "dispersed seasonal eco-center," which means a valuable food source spread out over much of the country at a certain time of the year. The result is that wilderness which didn't have bears in July or August is suddenly alive with bears in the fall. It also means the odds of a hunter having a bear encounter increase, just as they do for fishermen along a salmon stream in Alaska.

There is some anecdotal evidence that bears are actually drawn to the sounds of gunfire, having learned to associate a rifle shot with food. Many bear biologists believe there is some truth to this, and so too do outfitters like Vance. "I think they do (come to the sound of gunfire)," said Vance. "I've seen it in the Thorofare and I've seen it other places. You shoot and then within a few minutes, here's a bear. You know, why wouldn't they? You ring the dinner bell and we come to dinner. They are doing what we've habituated them to."

It's a nerve-wracking scene. A hunter has taken an elk and starts to work on the carcass, rolling up his sleeves, opening the body cavity with his knife, bending over and getting elbow-deep in blood and entrails. Suddenly there's a sound not unlike the pop of a .22 pistol and he looks up to see a bear charging, closing fast, ears flat against the skull, the hair on its back standing on end, and that sound—that eerie sound—of its teeth popping together. There is no warning sound, just the clack of tooth on tooth and a bear closing rapidly.

These are not bluff charges of surprised bears. "More often if you just come riding into an area and startle him, he may turn and come at you a little bit with what I've always known as a false charge, and that's totally different," said Vance.

The body language of a bluff charge is the main clue. "They don't have their ears back, their mouth's not open, and they aren't snapping their jaws. Their hair is not raised up and they just kind of make a run toward you and then they veer off to one side or another and they'll kind of look over their shoulder and will kind of lope off."

The other bear, the "I'm-not-bluffing-I-mean-business" bear, has another language. They may woof but more often it's just that popping sound of jaw and tooth. "Normally in my experience if one of them is woofing, that is a false charge because if they decide they are going to charge you they aren't going to waste any efforts on making noise," said Vance. "I think by snapping their jaws, they are giving you their last warning to 'Get out of the way, you are between me and what I want.' I think they are trying to give you one more warning to try and get away. You've got the hair up on your neck just like they do."

"They will put their ears back, they will be snapping their jaws, shaking their heads," said Vance. "There's no doubt in your mind and you don't have time to be getting your pepper spray out of a holster or anything."

For this reason, whenever a client takes an elk and before the field dressing begins, Vance takes out his pepper spray and lays it nearby, within reach. Vance has been charged three separate times by grizzly bears while he was field dressing an elk. Each time, the pepper spray was readily available instead of jammed into a holster, and each time, he's turned those bears with a blast of spray.

Each time Vance was charged, he dropped what he was doing, bent to the nearby pepper spray, thumbed off the plastic safety on the canister, and laid down a cloud of pepper spray in short bursts. The bear closed the distance faster than you can read this sentence. Two of the three times that Vance has been charged, he was alone—the client had been sent for the pack horses or help—but once, a client was with him. That client turned and ran while Vance stood by the dead elk. Running from a charging grizzly is the worst possible reaction because prey runs from predators.

"He was pretty scared, but it all turned out fine, I was between him and the bear," said Vance. So too was the red cloud of pepper spray. "All three times they ran right into it. I started making bursts of spray before they got that close and all three times as soon as they got that close the spray shut her down."

The final distance before a bear quit and took off was sometimes less than a half dozen steps. But the pepper spray worked every time and—unlike with a firearm—the bear wasn't wounded and still charging the shooter. In fact, Vance far prefers pepper spray to firearms. "We keep pepper spray in all the hunter tents and keep about four canisters of it in the cook tent," said Vance. "I tell the hunters that I prefer that they carry pepper spray rather than a handgun. They can certainly carry a handgun, that's their right, but we like to have them carry the pepper spray because you are just so much more effective with it than you are with a pistol if you have a close encounter. I carry a handgun but it's more for making noise or something like that, it's not for bear protection. My hand goes for the pepper spray before I ever think of going to a handgun for a bear."

Tug-o-war with a grizz

The load suddenly got heavier as a grizzly grabbed the other end

Wisconsin hunters Dick Thurk and Brad Bille were nervous. They had been awed by the mountains, by the vast forests, by the rivers. But they were on edge about bears. Grizzly bears. The people they had met in Wyoming weren't making it easy, either. It seemed they were getting warnings about bears everywhere they went:

"Better carry some bear spray."

"Got a handgun?"

"I wouldn't go out there with those bears."

"It's been dry this year, you better watch out because the bears will be hungry."

Gas stations, cafes, sporting goods stores—it didn't matter. Wherever they went, the hunters heard the same advice, starting almost as soon as they hit the state line.

Those words of caution ran through their minds as they dragged the carcass of the mule deer buck down the mountainside to their vehicle. Earlier that day, the men had climbed high into the forests above Grinnell Creek outside Cody to hunt deer. Thurk and Bille had never hunted in Wyoming before and they loved it, especially this bright October day in 2000. A few days earlier, it had snowed a few inches, but on this day it was warm and brilliant and the snow was melting rapidly, the kind of day that westerners call Indian summer.

But Thurk and Bille kept thinking about bears. It didn't help that they'd already seen some bears and that morning, Thurk had accidentally walked right up on a small bear—he didn't know if it was a black bear or a grizzly—and had been startled by it. They often checked their hip holsters for their canisters of bear spray.

They had climbed about a mile and a half up the drainage and sat down to watch a promising open slope for deer. Eventually a buck fed out into the open and Thurk was able to get a shot. They worked quickly to field dress the deer and now were dragging it down the trail to their truck.

"All the way down, we had both kinda been taking turns watching over our backs, you know because of what they had told us," said Thurk. "You know the stuff that runs through your mind."

It was late afternoon and the sun was tipping west, the light golden on the tallest peaks, the trail damp with snowmelt, the dragging easy. It looked like they would get back to the truck and then to camp well before dark.

The men were dragging the deer with a rope. They had each tied a loop into the rope and had shrugged themselves into this makeshift harness. They also grabbed the deer's antlers with a free hand and were making good time, but it was still awkward work, even going down hill, and the rifle slings and rope dug into their necks. Finally they rounded a bend and saw their vehicle below along the highway. An occasional car passed. They looked forward to getting back to camp to tell their buddies about the hunt.

The first thing the men noticed was an odd smell, one they thought might be left by some horses that had been on the trail. It was one of those thoughts that flash through your brain in a millisecond and sticks there.

The sequence of events is jumbled, but somewhere in those

last few seconds, the deer got harder to pull. Perhaps it was the little rise they were going up right before the final descent to the truck.

Maybe it was the smell, maybe it was pure instinct, but for some reason Thurk looked over his shoulder one last time before they tugged the carcass the final hundred yards to the truck. What he saw sent a shockwave through his body.

A grizzly bear was biting on and pulling the hindquarters of the deer they were dragging. It was a surreal moment and something that for a split instant Thurk thought he was imagining.

"I hollered 'Bear!' and I just kind of tipped—you know we had our guns and everything on our shoulders, our backpacks—and I just kind of tipped forward and pulled out of the rope and took off," said Thurk.

Thurk ran for the vehicle and while he was running, he was thinking that Bille, who was the young father of Thurk's grandson, would soon pass him as the two made tracks to the truck. "But he didn't pass me."

Instead, Bille was tangled up in the rope. All of this happened in an instant. "I didn't have the rope all the way over my neck yet when the bear pulled back. He pulled (the rope) right back down and knocked me into the ground," said Bille.

The bear was pulling on the deer carcass, trying to drag it back away from the road and, at the same time, dragging Bille in a bizarre tug-o-war. "I lost," said Bille. He struggled to get his bear spray out of its holster but dropped it in the melee.

Bille was yelling and Thurk finally heard him and stopped his dash to the truck. "I heard Brad holler, 'I'm caught in the rope,' and I turned around and I look and here the bear is dragging the deer and Brad on the ground.

"She didn't go very far with him, so I ran back then and I just raised the gun up and I had the scope turned up (in magnification) from when I shot the deer so I when I raised it up, all I see was black (in the rifle scope), so I put it back down to make sure I had the bear and not Brad, then I raised it again and I shot and she just kinda collapsed right there," said Thurk.

"Brad got out of the rope and we both kinda took off, you know because we didn't know whether she was dead or what she was going to do and she just kind of laid around the back of the deer," said Thurk.

But the bear was mortally wounded and not in pursuit of the men. They stopped and walked slowly back to the deer and the bear, rifles ready. She looked to be dead and they noticed blood pooling beneath her body. The entire episode had happened in an instant. One minute the men were dragging a deer to the road, sated by that feeling that comes near the completion of a successful hunt. The next minute they were in a strange struggle with a bear in a situation that was getting extremely dangerous.

The two men quickly retrieved their deer and threw it into the trailer. "We were only four miles from Yellowstone, so we went there and got hold of the rangers," said Thurk.

Yellowstone National Park Ranger Jesse Farias returned to the scene with the two men. They discovered that the bear was gone, but not far. Farias dispatched the bear quickly with his .30-06 rifle. Meanwhile, they waited for wardens with the Wyoming Game and Fish Department to arrive.

Craig Sax, the north Cody game warden, showed up and began to question the men. Shooting a grizzly bear, which is protected as a threatened species under the Endangered Species Act, is an act that calls for a thorough investigation. A federal investigator, Tim Eicher with the U.S. Fish and Wildlife Service, also had to be called in. But it quickly became apparent that the men's tale was so fantastic that it couldn't have been made up. That afternoon the men were cleared in the shooting and were able to take their deer back to camp.

There are several theories as to why the bear dared to go for the mule deer with the men right there. Investigators speculated that this bear, which was radio-collared and ear-tagged with number 316, may have been the offspring of 104, the oft-photographed sow grizzly who lived in relative harmony with people her whole life and who foraged beside the North Fork highway. If 104 was so used to humans and relatively tolerant of them, the logic follows that her daughter, 316, may have been that way as well and wasn't very alarmed by two hunters dragging a deer.

She was radio collared as a research bear, not a bear that had gotten into trouble, and was in fact being tracked as part of the overall study of grizzlies in the Yellowstone ecosystem. Some fifty bears in the ecosystem wear radio collars and researchers study their movements and extrapolate that data so they can get a feel for the entire population of grizzlies. This bear, a prime sow, had been captured near the Wyoming Game and Fish Department's Mormon Creek cabin right on the North Fork of the Shoshone River in 1998. That was her only capture. Until 316 ran across Thurk and Bille on October 17, 2000, she had no conflicts with humans, though she, like her probable mother, was seen and photographed beside the road.

Autumn is a time of extreme importance to all bears. They must eat as much as possible to accumulate fat for hibernation. During this feeding frenzy, called hyperphagia, the need to take on calories often outweighs the danger of humans. That's why bears take chances near hunting camps, cabins, and campgrounds. Getting food is the paramount instinct. For 316, that instinct turned out to be fatal.

"I don't think that she understood there was a couple of humans on the other end of that deer," said Sax. "That period of feeding is so important to them that it's really not unusual for bears to take chances. They were laying down a perfect scent trail as they dragged that deer down the trail and I'm sure she just crossed that trail and started to follow it. That's how we trap bears when we are moving them, we lay down a scent trail. I'm sure she just followed it thinking it was a wounded deer or whatever and never made the connection that there were humans on the other end."

She was in excellent shape, with good teeth and prime body condition, said Sax. She just needed more food before hibernation.

It's hard to overstate the importance of the fall feeding period for both black and grizzly bears. If they get enough food, they can get through hibernation and emerge in April in good shape. If they don't get enough food, they either starve in the den or have to emerge in the middle of the winter to look for more food. Meat is a big part of the picture.

"When eating fruits such as huckleberries or other foods that have a relatively low energy content, bears strive to eat over one-third of their body weight each day," said Dr. Charles Robbins, director of the Bear Research, Education and Conservation Program at Washington State University in Pullman. "Thus a 220-pound bear can eat as much as seventy pounds of fruit per day and will gain as much as a pound and a half per day. However, the same bear feeding on salmon can gain more than three pounds per day while eating approximately forty pounds of salmon. These daily gains that occur during fall hyperphagia provide enough stored energy for the fruit-eating bear to live three days during hibernation or the salmon-feeding bear to live seven days."

So even in a dry year, berries are less important to hibernation than meat. And 2000 was a very dry year with a poor berry crop. Little wonder that a deer was so tempting.

It took both men a while to get over the shock of having a hungry bear so close. Years later, both men get an occasional strange sensation when they are out in the woods hunting or fishing. It's a feeling as if something is watching them, and it has dogged Bille in particular. Yet both men plan to hunt in the West again someday. They feel a great respect for grizzlies and believe they are a crucial part of the ecosystem in north-western Wyoming.

"I'm all for them," said Bille. "I was on their territory, that's his land, not mine."

"That bear wasn't after us," added Thurk. "She wanted that deer and that's all she wanted."

Biography of a Grizzly, II

*Named after a fictitious grizzly, Little Wahb grows
legendary on cattle and sheep*

Jerry Longobardi is a loquacious man who speaks in quick
sentences and moves with the ease of a man comfortable in his
own skin and at home in the mountains. He likes to talk and he
talks mostly of the things he loves: mules, mountains, the cow
dogs he's owned, and wildlife. He rode saddle broncs in college
in Idaho, cowboyed in Arizona, punched cattle on the famed
Padlock Ranch out of Sheridan, Wyoming. Later, he rode for
the Flying D in Montana, a ranch that would become famous
when Ted Turner bought it, sold all the cattle, and brought
back bison.

Longobardi has guided, outfitted, rafted rivers, and worked
on the Alaska Pipeline. It's a career pattern that follows many
souls who have wild country in their veins. They are men and
women who want to live where it's hard to survive; they wait
tables, guide hunters, take dudes on trail rides, tend bar, row a
drift boat, help skiers onto chairlifts. Do this, do that, make a
living, get by, endure, work outside if you can because this is
what brought you here and keeps you here. Longobardi has
lived that life and enjoyed it.

In his early thirties, an age when most game wardens were
well along in their careers, Longobardi decided to become one.
He took the warden exam and became a rookie Red Shirt, the
nickname of Wyoming's warden force, whose typical uniform
includes red shirt, wool vest, and packer boots.

In 1991, Longobardi found himself stationed in the tiny burg of Meeteetse, a town that only a decade earlier had made national headlines for the discovery of a wild and very rare little carnivore called the black-footed ferret. Once thought extinct, a small colony of ferrets had been found in the sagebrush prairie outside Meeteetse, a testament to the wildness that still remains in this territory.

When Longobardi arrived in Meeteetse in May that year, his Ford F-250 filled to the top with all of his possessions and his heeler, Tess, riding shotgun, the locals were all saying that another native of the country no longer roamed the range, the grizzly bear. But that first summer in the country, Longobardi cut the tracks of a grizzly in Venus Basin in the Greybull River drainage. "So I knew that wasn't true," he said.

Of any country near Yellowstone National Park, the Meeteetse country was probably the most likely to be grizzly-free. Located on the extreme southeastern corner of what conservationists call the Greater Yellowstone Ecosystem, Meeteetse has long been livestock country, with huge chunks of range grazed for more than 100 years by cattle and domestic sheep. Bears in livestock country, especially bears with an appetite for mutton or beefsteak, don't last long. What's more, hunters intent on killing bears had been coming to the Meeteetse for more than a century. The Confederate Col. William Pickett owned a ranch on the Greybull River for years and did his best to keep the bear population shot down. He killed four grizzlies on just one moonlit night in 1883.

But in 1991, the country had much changed. The grizzly bear had been under the umbrella protection of the Endangered Species Act since the mid-1970s and hunters no longer could shoot them for any—or no—reason. Nor could a rancher legally shoot a grizzly bear, even if it was caught attacking a prized bull or lamb.

In 1992, Longobardi's second summer in new country, there were reports of a bear killing domestic sheep up on Carter Mountain. The herder wanted to unlimber his taped-up, ancient .30-30 rifle on the bear—black bears can be legally shot when caught in the act of whacking livestock—but Longobardi urged caution. "I remember saying, 'No, you better not do that, it might be a grizzly.'"

Longobardi and Tim Fagan, another warden whose district included the west side of Carter Mountain, bounced in a pickup clear to the head of Meeteetse Creek, towing a culvert bear trap. They thought they might catch the bear that was killing sheep.

Carter Mountain is the left thumb of a massive chunk of mountain that lies on the northwestern corner of Wyoming like a giant hand, palm down. If the fingers rest on Yellowstone National Park, then far south and a little east is the thumb that is Carter. There's a valley between the thumb and the index finger known as the South Fork, a country of stunningly beautiful and historic ranches set against tall mountains. Carter itself rises more than 12,000 feet high, some 6,000 feet above the valley floor below. And on the very top of the mountain was the last remaining band of domestic sheep, 1,800 yearling ewes owned by rancher Dave Grabbert. At tone time, many thousands of sheep had roamed the country, but dwindling prices and foreign competition had taken their toll on Wyoming wool growers.

Longobardi and Fagan never did catch the bear that summer, but the problems didn't go away. The next summer they got worse. Grabbert's herder—a different man from the previous summer and an on-again, off-again employee who sometimes went off and left the band to fend for itself—reported the first lost ewe in late June. Then another. And another. Some bear was taking one, sometimes two and even three sheep a week. The herder would find their carcasses buried in mounds of forest duff and report them back to Grabbert.

"It was a pretty frustrating situation because the bear just kept killing and kept killing and they wouldn't allow me to do anything," said Grabbert. "This thing was killing on us from the 28th of June through July, through August and into September, just a continual deal. I wasn't allowed to kill the bear."

What he could do was call Longobardi, who called Mark Bruscino, whose fulltime job with the department was to deal with bears and deal with people in bear country, a job that the bureaucracy gives the title "bear management specialist." For the better part of a month starting in early July, Bruscino and Longobardi tried to capture the bear that was killing sheep.

Although Longobardi might have had suspicions that the sheep-killing bear was a grizzly, both men initially thought it was more likely a black bear. It had been years since anyone had heard of a grizzly bear on Carter Mountain, and even though Longobardi had seen evidence of grizzlies in the Greybull River drainage, this was the very thin edge of their modern-day range. Finding a grizzly on Carter may not have been as long as the odds of discovering that the black-footed ferret was still kicking, but it was still very unlikely. Black bears, while less aggressive than their larger cousins, are nevertheless efficient sheep killers.

Then the men started cutting tracks in the mud along streams, and the tracks told the story as well as if they had been reading a book. There was no mistaking the square pad and long claws. There was a grizzly on Carter, not a very big one, but definitely a grizzly. Was this the bear that was taking sheep left and right?

In late July, Bruscino set up an Aldrich foot snare near a fresh sheep kill to answer that very question. The foot snare is a very effective and common tool in the live capture of bears. Comprised of quarter-inch, flexible steel aircraft cable anchored to a stout tree by a logging chain, the snare is virtually impossible for even a very large grizzly to break or chew apart. When set, the snare encircles an area on the ground about the size of the average dinner plate. A spring-loaded arm acts as a trigger. When the bear steps in the middle, the arm snaps and the snare tightens like a lariat around the foot.

In a few days, the trap was sprung and in the snare was a young male grizzly. He was the first grizzly on Carter Mountain in at least fifty years. "It was interesting because it was one of these 'grizzlies can't climb trees right?'" said Longobardi, "and when we were walking up to him he just ran right up that tree (that the snare was tethered to)."

Bruscino estimated the bear's weight and loaded his dart pistol with enough Telazol to put the bear to sleep. Telazol is a dissociative anesthesia that will knock a bear down for about forty-five minutes to an hour. Bruscino took aim and shot a four-cc dart into the bear's blond hide. In minutes, the little bear was fast asleep in the tree. Tree climbing hadn't been in Bruscino's original job description, but he went up and handed the bear down to Longobardi.

"He couldn't have weighed a hundred fifty pounds," said Longobardi. "He was just a cute little thing. He was just a little weaner."

Grizzly cubs are typically weaned as two-year-olds and young males will wander far and wide looking for new country. "He'd been kicked off (from his mother) probably that May or early June and he had parked himself right in the middle of a herd of domestic sheep and was living pretty high," said Bruscino.

This young bear captivated Longobardi, who has more than a touch of the romantic in his veins. As one might expect of a bachelor game warden in a small western Wyoming town, Longobardi is an avid reader. Two years previously, when he learned he would get his dream assignment in the Meeteetse area, he started to read everything he could about the country. One of the books he read was Ernest Thompson Seton's *Biography of a Grizzly*, a heavily anthropomorphized 1900 fictional tale of a grizzly bear on the Greybull River. Seton, who is at once lionized and vilified as a naturalist who heavily dosed his animal characters with emotions, spent some time in Meeteetse country during the same era that Col. Pickett was packing his Sharps .45-90 in the high country. While the book is definitely fiction, it is based partially on fact and is dedicated to the cowboys of the Palette Ranch who ranched next to Pickett. The centerpiece of Seton's book is a bear named Wahb, the sole surviving cub whose mother and siblings were shot by Col. Pickett.

Now, nearly a century later, another young grizzly was in the Meeteetse country, and Bruscino worked quickly on the dozing bear. This was not the era of Seton and Pickett. Grizzly bears these days are poked and measured and radio-collared and ear-tagged. Bruscino aged and measured the bear, tattooed the inside of its lip, and gave it a radio collar. The collar transmitted a signal to a receiver and was designed to expand and then fall off as the bear grew older and bigger. Bruscino made notes of the bear's condition and size. Then he gave the little bear a numbered ear tag. It was number 212, but to Longobardi and soon to most everybody in the country, it was Little Wahb.

While the men worked on the bear, Grabbert's herder showed up. The men discussed whether this was the bear that had been killing the sheep. If so, it would have to be moved out of the area. They talked back and forth and the herder finally decided that no, this wasn't the bear. They stood back as the drug slowly wore off. Longobardi snapped a picture of the groggy bear with a backdrop of some of the wildest country in the Lower Forty-Eight. Finally, Little Wahb staggered to his feet and ran for the timber. Bruscino and Longobardi both remember the herder's words as the bear left: "Well, maybe that was him."

It was ironic. A few minutes earlier they could have done something. They could have moved the bear far away to Yellowstone National Park or somewhere else in the ecosystem. Now all they could do was watch the drowsy young bear stumble off into the same country where he or some other bear like him had an appetite for sheep. Or maybe they wouldn't have done anything. At the time, Bruscino and Longobardi were themselves uncertain if they had captured the right bear. Even today, Longobardi, perhaps more so than Bruscino, is unsure if Little Wahb started out his livestock killing with those sheep on that mountain in 1993.

Nevertheless, the sheep continued to die. The most deadly incident came in late summer when a good portion of Grabbert's herd was found piled up dead at the bottom of a steep ravine. By this time, the herd was not getting the best of care from the man paid to tend them. Grabbert's herder had completely quit the country, and the sheep had drifted on their own out of the allotment into bighorn sheep country on North Pickett Creek. From all appearances, it looked as if the sheep had been pressed into a writhing, bleating mass and driven off what was essentially a cliff. In all, 133 sheep were scattered at the bottom of the gully. Could a bear have pushed them to their deaths? It was possible, but there was no sign of predation, and by the time the sheep were discovered, they had been dead quite some time.

Grabbert thought the sheep had been pushed off the cliff by a bear and so did the majority of the Wyoming Game and Fish Commission, which pays ranchers for livestock losses to grizzlies. In the end, the commission paid Grabbert for 160 sheep at $100 apiece. But when the sheep trailed off the mountain that fall, it was for the last time. Domestic sheep would not graze Carter in the future, ending a tradition that had spanned several decades and had started with the man that Grabbert's father had purchased the ranch from in the 1940s.

"You know Dave was a good guy," said Longobardi. "I asked Dave 'Hey, if I can get you an allotment in the Big Horns, would you move your sheep over there?' and we did and he did. And that was the end of the sheep on Carter Mountain, which with all the grizzlies we've got up there now we just could no way run sheep up there. It would be genocide."

Meanwhile, snow blanketed Carter Mountain and Little Wahb found a den high in the Pickett Creek drainage. His collar gave off a slow, steady signal that indicated he was deep in hibernation.

That winter Longobardi made several trips on skis into the North Pickett Creek patrol cabin that is owned by the department. "I knew he had a den up in Pickett Creek a couple of winters," said Longobardi. "You know that's kind of a hard thing when we start hunting these grizzlies is when you radio collar them and you get to know them kind of personally . . . and anyway, I'd just think about him laying up there in his den and I tried several times to find it and I never could."

Although it was the end of sheep on Carter Mountain, Grabbert converted his U.S. Forest Service grazing allotment from sheep to cattle at a rate of about one cow for every ten sheep. Since cattle aren't as suitable for high country grazing, he estimates the ranch lost about half of its summer range. That spring when Little Wahb came out of hibernation, Grabbert moved cattle onto the allotment. All around the mountain, other ranchers moved their cattle up the mountain onto private and public lands.

For that summer and the next several summers, it was fairly quiet on Carter Mountain. Cattle, like sheep, die for reasons other than grizzly bear attacks. They die from diseases, they die from eating the wrong thing, they injure themselves in rugged country, and they get bogged down in mud. They die for no apparent reason. Most of the losses are calves. Each year for the next three years, the surrounding ranches had a few losses to grizzly bears, with most of the losses being claimed by the TE Ranch over the mountain from Meeteetse.

Buffalo Bill Cody founded the historic TE in the 1880s. It sits on the South Fork of the Shoshone surrounded by rugged mountains on three sides. Charles Duncan, who served as Secretary of Energy under President Jimmy Carter, owns the TE today. It is managed by Curt Bales. Downstream, Curt's brother, Tom, ranches the Bales home place, and near Tom's ranch is the famous Hoodoo, which has been owned by Hunt Oil out of Dallas, Texas, since the 1940s. There are other ranches in the country as well, flanking all sides of Carter and running cattle nearly to the top of the mountain, home territory of Little Wahb. But by now he wasn't the only grizzly on the mountain.

Not long after Little Wahb was captured and then released, more grizzlies began to show up. "It seemed like Carter Mountain kind of came alive with grizzlies," said Bruscino.

It all went bad in 1997. That was the year that cattle started being killed on a regular basis. Not just calves but big yearlings, 800-pound yearlings that would be difficult for most predators to bring down. Sometimes a bear was taking down even bigger quarry. In 1996, the TE lost two calves and a mother cow weighing about 1,200 pounds to a grizzly at the head of Rock Creek.

Biologists figured one bear was doing the killing because the *modus operandi* was always the same. With one or two bites to the neck and withers, he could efficiently kill a yearling steer, and in less than a day he and the scavengers of the high country would have it cleaned up.

"We found a big, white yearling steer that probably weighed 800 pounds and he was just laying on the forest," said Grabbert. "You looked around him and there didn't seem to be anything obviously wrong with him. But then we examined just a little bit closer and there were these fang marks in his neck in front of his shoulder, just one bite, and he was dead."

That was early one morning. Twenty-four hours later, there was hardly enough left of the steer to toss into the bed of a pickup. "There was a head and some leg bones and the hide and some of the backbone and that's essentially what was left," said Grabbert. "Now he might have had some help, but that's a lot of meat for twenty-four hours from a fresh kill. It's almost unbelievable."

By this time, the radio collar around Little Wahb's neck had come off so the state trappers had no way of knowing if he was doing the killing. But they did have some suspicions based on Little Wahb's earlier history. Meanwhile, cattle losses kept mounting. Most were from the TE herd.

"I think he had killed nine yearlings on us that year," said Curt Bales. "That was one of the first years that we had a lot of problems. He was getting about one a week."

Bales was running the yearlings in Rock Creek pasture, a 3,000-acre piece of very rugged terrain that had been cow country for 120 years. Now it was grizzly country again, and that was causing Bales and his neighbors to change the way they operated.

"We was having to do a lot of riding," said Curt. "It's normally an area where we don't have to do a lot of riding, especially for yearlings, they kind of stay spread out and stuff. But quite often we was just trying to find the bear kills so we could get paid for them."

In order for a rancher to get paid for livestock losses to animals like grizzlies, there has to be sufficient evidence that the animal was killed and didn't just die. This evidence usually comes in the form of a hide that has tooth or claw marks and has to be reported to the department within fifteen days. This meant the cowboys had to find a fresh kill and skin it out. It could be a nerve-wracking job at best.

With thousands of acres to ride, many kills likely went undetected. Warden Tim Fagan estimates that by this time the bear was taking twenty cattle per year. Sometimes, the bear wasn't able to kill them. "We found a couple of yearlings that weren't dead, they were pretty chewed up and we had to destroy them," said Bales. "You could tell it was really a battle to actually kill them."

Whatever bear it was, it was exceedingly tough to catch. The grizzly would kill a yearling or a calf and eat as much of it as he could. If ranch hands didn't discover the carcass, it's likely he stayed on it as long as it took to consume it. But if there were a lot of human activity around the carcass, such as setting up a trap or snare, he'd be over the other side of Carter Mountain. For him, it was a quick hike, but for the state wildlife guys trying to capture him, it was a trek of almost 100 miles of dirt road and pavement as they circumnavigated the base of the big mountain.

"He'd be there for one night, maybe two nights, and then he'd leave because we set traps," said Fagan. "He'd just pull out. He would just work all back and forth across Carter Mountain, work clear to the other end of his territory, always moving away from people. But the way he killed, you knew it was probably the same bear who was doing it."

In fact, few people ever saw the bear during his entire stay on the mountain—not the ranch hands, not the wardens, no one. Those who did, saw him only after he'd been fooled, caught in a trap first as a young bear and then late in 1997 when they finally caught him again.

In late summer that year, Fagan and Chris Queen, a bear management officer working with Bruscino, found another kill—a calf—out in the sagebrush. This time, they were determined to trap him. "I just took a deep breath and said, 'Okay, we are going to catch this guy,'" said Fagan.

They worked hard on the culvert trap, covering it with sagebrush, putting dirt in the bottom. "We just made it look like a cave."

They worked quickly, baited the trap with the calf, and pulled out. During the night, the grizzly came back to the kill site. He walked around and around and around the culvert trap, beating down a path in the grass and brush as he checked out the bait, smelling the dead calf inside. Finally he went in and the steel door slammed down and locked behind him. Bear 212—Little Wahb—had made a mistake that would eventually lead to his demise.

Early the next morning Fagan and Queen checked their trap. Since Little Wahb was tagged, they had to find out the bear's history. When they learned this bear had been suspected of killing Grabbert's sheep in 1993, they had to decide whether to move the bear out of the region or destroy him. Under the agreement of the Interagency Grizzly Bear Committee—a group of state and federal agencies in and around the Yellowstone country—male grizzlies in their prime are given only one chance. Technically, if Little Wahb had been doing the killing in 1993, he already had his one chance and the guidelines called for his removal. But the guidelines also leave some flexibility for the people on the ground. It's a complicated series of decisions that include federal and state authorities, conference calls, and records checking. All the while, there's a bear in the trap on a hot summer day, and there's concern for the animal's well being.

Fagan argued against letting the bear go. "Not that I necessarily wanted to kill him, but man this guy had frustrated the hell out of us. I said we are never going to catch him again and he's going to come back no matter where we put him because he's been in here since he was a little guy. So there was a lot of frustration on our part."

Eventually, a decision was made to give Little Wahb a second chance. He'd be moved deep into Yellowstone National Park and radio collared again. Additionally, 212 would have a transmitter implanted in his abdomen, a transmitter that would likely outlast the radio collar and give off a signal no matter where the bear went or what he did.

Once again 212 got a dose of Telezol, and he was measured and recorded. No longer was Little Wahb little. Now he weighed more than 400 pounds.

The internal transmitter is about the size and shape of a hotdog and is planted in the abdominal cavity. Connective tissues gradually grow around the transmitter and hold it in place. While he was anesthetized at the trap site, a veterinarian surgically implanted the transmitter. The incision was sewn up and Little Wahb was ready for new country. Now biologists could track his movements from the ground and from the air. Unless something happened to both the collar and the internal transmitter, there would be no hiding for the elusive grizzly.

Little Wahb was released on Blacktail Plateau—a sage and grass plateau in the heart of Yellowstone. It was August and he was deep in the park, miles away from Carter Mountain, surrounded by elk and bison, with rivers and ridges between himself and his home country. By next spring he was back on Carter Mountain killing cattle.

He had improved his killing efficiency, bringing down the occasional 1,200-pound cow along with yearlings and calves. It wasn't random killing for the fun of it, but killing to live, to survive. In every case, unless he was pushed off the kill by human activity, he ate most of the carcass.

He was killing on the TE, on the Hoodoo, on the Bales ranch, on the Grabbert ranch, and on others. Estimates vary, but most agree that Little Wahb was pulling down about one calf, yearling, or mother cow every week, and sometimes two per week.

He wasn't alone. Little Wahb may have been the pioneer to reclaim the mountain, but grizzlies were now entrenched on it. Some were apparently following Little Wahb and dining on his kills—several were caught by game wardens while they were trying to get 212. Some may have been doing their own killing. On the Tom Bales ranch, only about ten miles out of downtown Cody, a young grizzly killed three 4-H lambs that were being raised by Tom's daughter. The bear killed them right in their ranch yard, within 200 feet of their house. On the other side of the mountain, Grabbert found a 1,800-pound bull that was badly chewed and clawed by a bear. The bull would later recover.

Little Wahb's days were numbered. With the radio transmitters, the wardens—now joined by a federal wildlife damage agent named Jim Pehringer—could get a pretty good fix on his location. With an airplane they could pick up the signal and pinpoint the bear's general locale and then move in on the ground with hand-held receivers.

Yet catching 212 was like trying to net a shadow. Wherever a kill was discovered, Longobardi, Bruscino, Fagan or Pehringer would set up culvert traps and foot snares, but Little Wahb was now wise to traps. In fact, he would never be trapped again. A decision was made to try and shoot him.

"You know, I hated to have to do it, but I knew his end was near," said Longobardi. "There was a lot of cows dying."

Still, Little Wahb was nearly ghost-like. Once Longobardi, Bruscino, and Pehringer tried to pin down the bear in a patch of timber. Using the radio receiver, they quietly slipped through the woods, rifles ready.

"We knew he was within 300 or 400 yards and there we are sneaking along and it was pretty exciting," said Longobardi, but Little Wahb just slipped away. The men never even saw him. All of a sudden, the signal got weaker and then disappeared all together. No bear, no signal. Gone.

"He would just sneak away," said Longobardi. "None of this charging and eating you and that kind of stuff. He didn't want anything . . . he was a good secretive bear."

Little Wahb was the kind of bear that a human could have walked right past and never known he was there. In fact, Longobardi felt he did just that one summer day. "I was in North Meeteetse crick and here I was walking along and all of a sudden I see a dead elk covered and bear shit everywhere and a crashing in the trees and it was probably him. You know, he just didn't want anything to do with people."

Another time the men found a dead calf far out in the open on the Grabbert ranch. Nearby was a sheep corral they could use as a blind. Working from the back of Pehringer's pickup truck and being careful to not leave much scent around, Longobardi was able to get a rope on the carcass. They dragged it to a telephone pole within 100 yards of the corral.

Little Wahb was close. Pehringer and Longobardi set up with their rifles while Bruscino monitored the bear. Late that afternoon, a bear came in.

"The whole country is full of cattle and this was just so interesting." said Longobardi. "You think that cows are scared of grizzlies? Huh unh. I would have loved to have this on film. All of a sudden we look up and here comes this big beautiful silvertip right down the ridge and I'm like, 'Oh shoot, here he comes.' All the cows look up like, 'Yeah, we see grizzlies all the time,' and go back to eating.

"The grizzly walks right through the cows and they didn't even step out of the way. He hits where the calf was before I drug it, puts its nose to the ground just like a bloodhound, follows it right to the telephone pole and starts eating."

Pehringer and Longobardi look to Bruscino for the signal to shoot. The bear turns sideways to the corral, providing a perfect shot. They look to Bruscino, they look to the bear. "Mark just sits there and looks at us and shakes his head," laughed Longobardi. "It isn't Little Wahb. It was another grizzly."

The men decided to watch the show for a while. "All of a sudden about ten cows and calves in a group and with a little black baldy calf in the lead walk up like they are egging him on, like they are going to count coup on that grizzly. Those cows and calves with that calf in the lead are like, dunt . . . dunt . . . walking right up to that grizzly and the calf gets like fifteen feet from the grizzly and the grizzly turns around and looks at the calf and runs off! And then the bear turns around and you can see the grizzly go like, 'Wait a minute, I'm a grizzly' and he turns around and runs (back at the cattle) and they all scatter and he goes back to eating and five minutes later here they come again. Curious. Walk right up to the grizzly. Curious. It was the darndest thing you've ever seen."

In the meantime, Little Wahb left the area and the cattle killing continued elsewhere. Throughout the next three summers, the killings continued. So did the attempts to kill or catch Little Wahb.

One time a pilot who was monitoring signals from radio collars was able to find Little Wahb in a finger of timber that opened onto a sage bench. It looked like the perfect set up. The timber gave way to open sagebrush on three sides and was only about fifty acres in size. Bruscino reasoned that if someone could push through the timber, perhaps he could drive 212 into the open where a shooter could take out the grizzly. Fagan and Bruscino got on their horses while Pehringer set up with his rifle on the other end. With Bruscino operating the receiver, they pushed through the timber. Meanwhile, the pilot turned the airplane in slow circles overhead, tracking the bear as well.

It was a method of hunting that didn't appeal to any of the men. "If you think about it, it was so unfair to him, I mean we could track him on the radio," said Fagan.

Despite the odds against him, Little Wahb slipped out once again. As Bruscino and Fagan moved through the stand of timber, Pehringer waited. And waited. And waited. The pilot radioed down to Pehringer: "Well, he's already fooled you, he's behind you."

Apparently Little Wahb "got to the edge of the timber and turned around and he went back between us," said Bruscino. "We never saw him." He had eased past the riders and gone back through the timber and up the mountain into the deep woods. "This bear had been around cows and cowboys so long it was just no big deal for him to slip right past us," said Pehringer.

The saga continued. Another time, Pehringer camped out on the bear all day long, waiting for him to come out into the open from a little patch of timber. Starting early in the morning and using the receiver, he waited where he could get a good shot when the bear came out. The bear never moved and when darkness fell, Pehringer went home. The next day, the bear was gone. While riding past the spot where Little Wahb had been, Pehringer's horse spooked. The scattered remains of another kill lay in the timber.

Other bears were enjoying the spoils as well. While trying to catch Little Wahb, Longobardi and Pehringer snagged several grizzlies and one black bear. One of the grizzlies was a massive beast. Longobardi videotaped the bear while it was in the snare. During its struggle to free itself from the trap—the beauty of the snare is that it doesn't hurt the bear—the bear nearly chewed down the entire anchor tree, a spruce that was more than a foot in diameter. This bear, like 212, wanted nothing to do with humans. The videotape shows the bear lunging away from the men, never offering to charge, hiding behind the tree until it is finally tranquilized and released.

As usual, Little Wahb was somewhere else. It was a situation that was completely frustrating to the men.

"He just did what a bear does," said Fagan, "but you know as far as people, he just avoided people, so that was the sad part of it, that really bothered me. He frustrated a lot of people. There were times that you just had no life because you were trying to deal with him. I mean we could track him on the radio and we'd still have a hell of a time catching up with him. He just eluded us for so long (that we were thinking) either we're not very good, or he's very good."

In the spring of 2000, Little Wahb spent a lot of time on the northwest side of Carter Mountain, killing several cattle on the Tom Bales ranch. Still, no one could capture him.

"He was pretty relentless on getting away," said Tom Bales. "I don't think the bear would have ever caused much human problems, you know as far as that goes. I guess unless you had him cornered or something along those lines or was on his kill or something."

In the fall, as the cattle were moved back down the mountain, Little Wahb followed his food source. It was in the low open country, with only scattered patches of timber, that Little Wahb made his final mistake.

While on another routine flight, a pilot picked up the signal from 212 in an aspen patch in the middle of sagebrush. This time, there was no large stand of timber for escape. The pilot radioed Pehringer, who moved in and set up with his rifle while the airplane moved overhead.

Fall in the Wyoming high country is like nothing else on earth. The sky seems scrubbed and it's as if the whole world is pure and clean and true. Everything is brilliant, crisp, from the scent in the air to the sharp wildness of bull elk's bugle. October 3, 2000, was that kind of day.

From his stand, Pehringer counted six huge bull elk bedded down in the same aspen patch as Little Wahb. The yellowed aspens shimmered in the breeze, crystalline. When Pehringer was ready, the pilot dipped the plane down over the aspens and flushed Little Wahb from his bed.

"He headed up the trail right toward me, came busting out to the edge of the timber where there were two large pine trees right where the trail came into the open, running really fast," said Pehringer. "He stopped and stood up."

When Little Wahb stood up, Pehringer pulled the trigger. The bear flipped over and ran back into the timber, and died. "It was a pretty sad deal," said Pehringer. "It made me feel kind of bad for quite a while."

Although the bear was now dead, the legend of Little Wahb was about to grow. Had he lived in another century, he would truly have been king of the mountain, pulling down bison and elk and living as bears did before the time of the white man. But Little Wahb lived and died in a new millennium.

Only eight or nine years old, the grizzly was immense. Had he lived another decade—many grizzlies live well into their twenties—he would have been record-setting. Pehringer and Bruscino were able to winch the carcass into the back of a pickup truck and take it to Cody. At the Wyoming Game and Fish Department's regional office there, they attempted to weigh the bear, but it bottomed out a scale that went to 500 pounds. Using another scale, they finally estimated the bear's weight at more than 800 pounds. The fat on 212's rump was more than six inches thick and his teeth were in excellent shape. Grizzlies that forage for roots and insects often have poor, ground-down teeth. As a result of his meat diet, Little Wahb's teeth were long and perfect.

By this time the word was out and ranchers and spectators from all over the Cody country came to see Little Wahb. There was little jubilation; a quiet respect for the bear seemed to permeate the air. Some ranchers called Pehringer to thank him for killing the bear, but it was a bittersweet moment for him and all the other men who had been involved.

"It really bothered me when we killed the Wahb," said Fagan. "I don't know if I would have wanted to be the one killed him. I wanted him gone, but I didn't want him dead I guess."

Longobardi, who calls the story of Little Wahb "a modern-day wildlife tragedy," was on the other side of the mountain when Little Wahb was killed. "I'm kind of glad I wasn't there, to be honest with you," said Longobardi.

But Little Wahb was just the first of many grizzlies in the country, said Longobardi. "You know, not to lessen his life any more, but we were thinking, we're going to set the (grizzly bear recovery) program back (by taking Little Wahb out) and holy smokes, I probably got fifty of them (now). Still, every time you gotta kill a bear, it just makes me sick. I'm kind of philosophical. There's a billion people on earth and all these animals just want to be left alone. He was just a bear, just trying to make a living."

The re-emergence of grizzlies on Carter Mountain has drastically changed the way of life for those humans who make their living there. Both Tom and Curt Bales were raised in the country and camped all over the mountain when they were children, but today they are afraid to let their own children do the same because of the bears. Bears routinely come down into the TE hay meadows each spring. Bears travel up and down the river corridor of the South Fork, and when the ranch's owners come out from Houston during the summer, they carry bear spray with them at all times. "When I was a kid growing up (in the 1960s and 70s) I can remember seeing two black bear on that mountain and now there's bear all over," said Curt.

When Little Wahb was taken out of the population, the cattle losses tailed off considerably, said Curt. In 2002, the TE only confirmed one calf as a grizzly kill.

The community of Meeteetse reveled in the legend of Little Wahb. A taxidermist mounted Little Wahb in a life-sized mount and it is the most popular attraction at the Meeteetse Museum. His story is told on a plaque on the mount, as well as on a menu at a local restaurant. A billboard on the north end of town carries his portrait and name.

The story of Little Wahb is a story of a bear trying to get by in the modern world. "Ninety percent of his range was in multiple use country outside of wilderness," said Longobardi. "He spent a lot his time within twenty miles of downtown Cody and fifteen miles of Meeteetse.

"I got a picture of him laying there on a canvas tarp (as a young bear in 1993) and waking up and looking around him at all those big mountains. I always look at that picture with all that big country all around him and the world just still wasn't big enough for him."

Angels don't leave tracks

A trail runner in Grand Teton National Park is run down
by a grizzly

Long-distance runner Michael Dunn was in the zone. It was one of those special days that come along all too rarely. Some days, it seems as if you have sand in your legs, as if the trail drags you down. But then there are the rare days when you think you can run forever, your muscles and sinew and bones all connecting, everything clicking, just going.

Dunn was having one of those exceptional days, "like there was a bungee cord pulling me along," said Dunn. "Give me more, I hope this doesn't end, just go and go."

Looking back now, Dunn thinks it was too good, too perfect, too ideal. And he thinks he'd been warned. That morning he shrugged off a feeling of uneasiness as he hit the trail between Emma Matilda and Two Ocean lakes in Grand Teton National Park. He thought it might be the same feeling that had haunted him the day before.

The previous morning Dunn had one of the best workouts of his life, but it was a morning that started out slowly, one of those legs-of-lead dawns. The trail had been muddied from night rain and the footing was tenuous. Fog hugged the ground, but as Dunn ran, it faded and a cast of light shone through. Deep into that run, the clouds parted and before Dunn in the light of one of the most beautiful sunrises he'd ever seen, rose the 13,770-foot summit of Grand Teton. An avid outdoorsman, Dunn had once climbed that mountain, but from this vantage, he was humbled, dwarfed, in its presence. Without thinking about it and completely out of character, he fell to his knees and gave a prayer of thanks for that beautiful morning.

Now it was a day later, August 14, 1994, and he felt like he was flying down a trail that he'd never explored before.

Every year, the park pulled the Dunn family north almost like that same bungee cord that now pulled Michael down the trail. They explored the park's many trails, climbed to the top of its tallest peak, watched sunrises and sunsets in the Tetons for summer after summer. A lifelong westerner, Michael knew almost every corner of the park except the trail on the southeastern corner that went from near Jackson Lake Lodge back into Two Ocean and Emma Matilda lakes. That was a trail that he had never been on before and one that he had vowed to investigate. For Dunn there wasn't a better way to explore that part of the park than an early morning trail run.

Dunn was addicted to long-distance running. Already he had some twenty marathons under his belt. However, trail running was relatively new to him. He was embracing it completely, especially this summer of 1994. Running down trails, over streams, and beneath vistas like he'd experienced the previous morning sure beat pounding the pavement, breathing in exhaust fumes from passing cars and getting shin-splints from concrete and asphalt. He was preparing for the St. George, Utah, marathon in a couple of months and this run seemed like the perfect training exercise.

Dunn was lost in the run, flittering random thoughts, sometimes thinking of nothing at all but the fluid motion of legs and arms working in harmony. He listened to the sound of his own breath, to the drumming of his feet on the trail, to the stillness of the morning, to the quiet sounds of the wilderness, to the dense forest of lodgepole and willow. He was deep into the run, perhaps eight or nine miles into it and about to loop around Two Ocean Lake and start back toward the bridge on the highway where he'd parked his car. It was so quiet, so peaceful, so perfect.

Suddenly a colossal noise behind Dunn broke his concentration. It was a sound like a clap of thunder, like a couple of trees breaking in half, a huge crash that was completely out of context with the calmness of the morning. It made Dunn leap into the air and look over his shoulder.

There, moving faster than he could ever imagine something so large moving, was a grizzly bear.

"At first, it was one of those blink your eyes kinds of things because you can't believe it," said Dunn. "You can tell it's a bear right away and as he runs, there's just not only speed but he's fixed on a target like a missile coming in." The target was Dunn.

In seconds Dunn's brain registered a dozen different details and thoughts. The bear was closing fast, less than thirty yards away. It exploded from a patch of brush, intersected the trail, and charged up the trail after Dunn.

"I could clearly see his jowls were open, his hair—which was kind of a weird color which had tints of gray in it but was almost a deep auburn color—was all bristled out and his ears were laid back. It was so clear how determined he was. The thing I could see as he was coming at me was every time that his head would drop a little bit, you could see the outline of the hump between his shoulder blades and that's when I thought, 'Aww, this is not just a bear, but it's a grizzly bear you are dealing with.'

"Your first instinct is you want to run, you want to yell, you want to do everything. I actually started into a run, because that was my instinct. You know you want to get out of there. You turn to run and then you look right back and you think, 'You are not going to outrun this bear.'"

These were the split-second thoughts and observations of the human brain in high gear. In reality, there wasn't time to do anything but brace for the impact as the bear charged up the trail and into Dunn. In an instant, Dunn was flying off the trail in a cloud of dust and blood.

"I remember just immediately screaming," said Dunn. "You are screaming and trying to fight and swing your arms and kick your legs."

The bear tore into Dunn as if he were a toy instead of a six-foot tall, 170-pound man in top condition. "The bear was just so fast, so agile," said Dunn. "(He was) rolling me around and it's probably a feeling similar to being in a washing machine. This bear is just handling me like a rag doll. Just throwing me everywhere and just biting and clawing and really, really mad. Well I don't know if mad is the word, but very, very agitated obviously."

Dunn fought as best he could, kicking and screaming and punching. Much of the time he spent on his stomach with the bear biting and raking his back and legs. The mauling seemed endless.

"I remember at one point I was down, I guess I was on my stomach side, and there was a little root just sort of growing there and I remember saying, 'I'm going to hang onto this, just really hunker down here, just really hold on as tight as I can,'" said Dunn. "But when he wanted to move me, he just ripped me out of there. (I guess) I could have held on and dislocated both shoulders. That's probably the most overwhelming thing, not just their size, but physically it's just such a mismatch, they are just so strong."

Dunn relied on instinct and that instinct told him to fight. Eventually, though, he realized that it was hopeless because of the bear's strength. He had no bear spray—backcountry travelers in 1994 had only just begun to discover and use pepper spray—and he was clad only in shorts and a t-shirt. With its long claws and teeth, the bear just flayed him.

"It's just going on and on and I remember realizing that this is it," said Dunn, "that you are going to die. And that was the weirdest feeling to be honest with you . . . this is the day you are going to die and it is just so odd. I guess you do what you do, you think about your family and your kids and your wife and that sort of thing. I just thought, 'I hope they find the body, so they have some sort of resolution to this,' because I just thought it's just going to tear me up and eat me because that's how intense it was at that point."

Whenever he could, Dunn would punch or kick at the bear. The bear spun him from one side to the other, biting sometimes, raking with its claws other times. Finally, one of those swipes from a paw caught Dunn in the face and a single claw went inside his mouth. With the claw now lodged like a fish-hook beneath Dunn's tongue and over his lower teeth, the bear began to pull back. Since the bear was on Dunn's back and he was face down in the dirt and forest duff, he couldn't roll with it. Instead, the bear twisted his head back, painfully and un-naturally.

"I realized 'Oh my gosh, he's trying to take my head off,' so I really fought and resisted," said Dunn. "I pulled back as hard as I could but he was pulling with his one claw and I'm pulling against him and I remember it got so bad that I'm pulling back and my upper back and all my neck and shoulder muscles just started to vibrate, shake really horribly because they couldn't contract and hold that much more."

Eventually, his head twisted around so far that the claw slipped out. As the claw slipped, it laid open Dunn's face as if he'd been cut by a very sharp fillet knife. "It just sliced right through my cheek . . . the claw bounced into my right temple and bounced into that temple bone and it dragged just above my ear, just barely missed my ear and then came out the back of my head. It really cut me all the way along just the top of my ear, literally almost scalping me in the process."

Now, almost exactly twenty-four hours after he had given a prayer of thanks, he realized it was time to ask for something. He said it aloud: "God, I need your help and I need it now."

Immediately Dunn realized that what he was doing was all wrong. The words, "play dead," flashed into his brain. He shouldn't be fighting the bear. "I remembered all of my good training in backcountry stuff, and I thought, 'Wait a minute, you've got to play dead.'"

So he did. He collapsed, pulling himself into the fetal position and covering up as best he could. The result was instantaneous. The bear stopped mauling him.

Dunn lay on his right side and the bear lay across him. He could hear the bear breathing and its breath was in his face. But the grizzly was looking around, staring intently into the forest as if something had suddenly distracted it. Dunn watched the bear as well as he could, ready for the mauling to start again.

"The weird thing is that his whole tone sort of changed at that point," said Dunn. "All of a sudden he was looking around like something was really bothering him. The bear just kept looking toward the woods and the bear started looking around almost as if he was really, really nervous about something that was out in the woods."

Dunn watched the bear turn its head and peer into the forest. The bear wasn't interested in him any more. "(I didn't know if) maybe God was somehow distracting this bear or angels were or whatever . . . but I just saw the bear sort of distracted and I decided—of all the smart things—that I would try to hit him. I would hit him in the snout."

Dunn was pinned down by the bear. He was lying on his

right arm, but his left was free, so he measured the distance to the bear's nose and calculated his punch.

"I took this big swing and fortunately didn't hit him in the face. I missed because I had some blood in my face I guess, but my punch came around and hit him in probably what would be the upper bicep area," said Dunn.

Even though the punch was with all of his strength, the bear didn't even flinch. Instead, it kept looking intently into the woods. "I was sort of hoping for this huge reaction, you know it would just sting him so bad, it would shock him or something and he didn't do anything. He was just really, really consumed with something that was unnerving him out in the forest."

So Dunn covered up and went back to playing dead.

"Within a couple of minutes, he suddenly just got up and took off down the trail really fast," said Dunn. The bear left so quickly that it showered Dunn with rocks and dirt and pine needles as it left.

Then the bear stopped thirty or forty yards away, rose onto its back feet and stared into the forest. "It turned around and I thought he was actually coming back for me," said Dunn.

Instead, the bear just stood on its hind legs. Dunn was in awe at the size of the grizzly as it stood there. "He just sort of, almost like a trained circus bear, he just sort of pirouetted his way around. He was like really looking for whatever this thing was that bugged him so much out in the woods," said Dunn. "And I didn't know it, but he was totally done with me. He knew I was not a threat and he came back down on all fours."

The bear woofed and then just took off into the thickest part of the forest towards whatever it was looking at "and that was the last I saw of him."

Dunn, who is a writer and producer, later wrote an account of the attack. In that account, he noted: "There was definitely something out there, even though later official investigations would reveal that there was no other animal or human evidences in that part of the forest that day—proving, if nothing else, that angels really don't leave footprints."

But it was while lying there in a pool of blood that Dunn really started to get scared. And he started to feel pain. During the mauling, he hadn't felt any real pain, but now he realized he was in pretty sorry shape. He was a long way from help, he was torn and bleeding, and the bear that had nearly killed him was still in the woods. He rose to a sitting position and assessed his injuries, pulling back into the recesses of his mind to remember some backcountry first aid training he'd had.

The worst wound was on his right thigh where the bear's claws had ripped deeply and parted the big muscles into two strips. Dunn could see the white of his femur down there through all the torn muscle and blood. "I started the process of like, 'Okay, how do we get out of here? Like how are you going to do this?' He had with a claw—just literally like a backhoe going to work—removed all the muscle and flesh all the way down to the femur bone . . . and the two parts of my leg, I didn't even know how they were staying together."

He took off what was left of his t-shirt and tore it into strips that he packed into the wound and wrapped around it. He did what he could for the other wounds as well. Then he staggered to his feet and started off down the trail. The bear had gone into the woods, so he decided that he'd go back down the trail toward his car eight or nine miles away.

"What I knew was I wanted to survive," said Dunn. "I wanted to get out of there and get help and I thought about it and just made a real quick decision on which way to go.

"I was just sort of dragging this leg, I really couldn't walk properly so I just was dragging it. At first I was really just yelling 'Hellllllllppppphhhh!' but I couldn't even make a sound, just these moans," said Dunn. "I went down a little further and

I look back and there was this trail of blood following me and I'm screaming and yelling out there and I thought, 'This bear is not going to need to be Daniel Boone to come and find me again.' Then it dawned on me also—you sort of get progressively smarter as you go along—I realized that I've really got to conserve all of the energy I have to get out."

It was like a scene out of a low-budget slasher movie. His scalp was in strips and blood poured down his face. His leg was mangled and all he could do was drag it along. After a mile of this shuffling, dragging gait, Dunn reached a clearing. He was completely exhausted and he was cascading blood. He needed to lie down and rest, but instead of lying down in the soft grass to the side, he laid right across the rocky trail, thinking, "If I die here, somebody's going to have to march across my body to miss it. I'm not going to be laying out there."

By now he was in tremendous pain. "I don't know how long I was there, maybe a half hour, forty minutes, and as I was laying there I kind of heard like people talking," said Dunn. "(I thought) I was kind of hallucinating and I thought, 'No, that's not people talking.'"

But it was.

On a ridge above the clearing, Dunn could see three people. "They are just standing there and they are talking and because of the way I was laying on this trail, I know they can see me, and I'm just thinking, 'What are they doing? I mean, help me.' All of a sudden, I got this thought that these people aren't going to help me, they are going to move on and if they do, you are dead. So I got myself up and I yelled as loud as I could," said Dunn. "'You've got to help me I've been attacked by a bear and I'm bleeding to death. I need your help!' And they didn't do anything. It was just so weird and then all of a sudden all three of them just kind of broke toward me on a dead run and I kind of relaxed."

Later, he asked them what they were doing. They said they could see that he was badly injured, but they didn't know where the attack had occurred and thought the bear might still be in the area, so they were surveying the scene.

"They didn't want to go in and be dessert," said Dunn. "They thought the bear was still in the area. So you can't blame them."

Jim and Linda Bourett and Trisha Lavin, all from nearby Jackson, were out for a day hike when they came across Dunn. Jim Bourett ran for help while the two women stayed behind to help.

"He was pretty cut up. I never felt like he was going to die or anything because he sounded so strong and he seemed really pretty calm," Lavin later told the *Casper* (Wyoming) *Star-Tribune*.

A ranger arrived and tended to the wounds. Dunn remembers that the ranger's first aid kit was soon exhausted. A helicopter from St. John's Hospital in Jackson was scrambled, and Dunn, although in extreme pain, was the first person to hear it.

"I said 'Here it comes' and they said, 'No, no, it's not' and here it appeared right over the tree tops," said Dunn. "It's one of those with one of those clear plexi domes on the back so you are laying on this stretcher looking up at the blue sky and the sun and it just took off and it's a little bit like, 'Wow, this feels like when you are dying or going to heaven.' It was just sort of an amazing feeling, very peaceful."

Dunn's wounds stunned the doctors at the hospital. "You see wounds like that from motorcycle accidents at ninety miles per hour, car accidents, that kind of thing," Dr. Paul Fenton told the *Casper Star Tribune*. "It was weird, it was like watching a great, incredible act of nature take place. You're almost in awe . . . You just couldn't believe that something could do that to him, that some animal or some force of nature could do that to him."

On Dunn's back, the doctor could see a clear imprint of one of the bear's paws in the bruised and damaged tissue. "He put his paws into him and it dug right down to his ribs," said Fenton. "Just the strength and sheer power of him was incredible."

The most serious injury was Dunn's leg where the bear's claws had completely removed a large portion of the sartorius muscle, the longest muscle in the human body. The bear's claws had also done something remarkable in that wound. The claws had traveled exactly parallel to the femoral artery, actually cutting this major artery out of the connective tissue and muscle in Dunn's leg and laying it back down in the open wound without puncturing or tearing the artery itself. Had the claws taken a different path or angle, they would have ripped it apart, and if the femoral artery is severed, a person will die in minutes. Dunn knew he was extremely lucky.

"Obviously, those claws can rip anything to shreds," said Dr. Fenton. "And how he never touched the artery is still beyond me. If the bear would have hit the artery he would have bled to death right there."

The wounds were full of pine needles and dirt. The initial cleaning of the wounds and the subsequent surgery took five hours. Dunn underwent another surgery three days later. He had sixteen major wounds and required some 300 stitches. "I was literally just quilted back together," said Dunn.

During this time, Dunn was surrounded by heroes, from his wife and three children, to the doctors and friends who gathered around him. There was also a tremendous amount of attention from officials and media since this was the first mauling by a grizzly bear in Grand Teton National Park's sixty-five-year history.

Dunn focused on getting back on his feet, although he thought he might never walk again. After a two-week stay in St. John's, he was back in his home in Park City. There he started a very long road to recovery. Sixty-five days after the attack, the wound in his thigh finally closed and Dunn took his first steps. Now the milestones in his life weren't marathon runs. They were the first time after the attack that he was able to walk, the first time he walked to the end of his driveway, and, five months after the attack, the first time he ran a mile.

Friends pushed him, telling him he'd be running the next year in the 100th running of the Boston Marathon. Eventually, Dunn's runs started to go longer and he realized his body was compensating for the severe injury to his thigh. He really could run. Slower. Less gracefully. But he could run. And so he did.

Fourteen months after the attack, Dunn entered the St. George Marathon, which would be a qualifying race for the Boston. As he stood in the starting line, he wondered just what he was doing and doubts rose. But he ran anyway. Twenty-five miles into the race with one mile to go, he rounded a bend and saw his family and friends cheering. His boys, Jeff, eight, and Brady, ten, screamed, "Dad, you are going to make it!" and ran the last mile with him.

"Tears are rolling down my face," said Dunn. "It was almost like coming out of the woods again. (I'm thinking) I can't believe that I've survived this. I was really just happy to be alive."

The attack was life-changing in many ways. Shortly after recovering he left a full time job with an advertising agency and started his own company. He also swung back into the routine of long-distance running and the dedication that entails. Much of the training was on trails in remote mountain country, including Grand Teton National Park. But not alone.

"I've gotten smarter about being in bear country. I run with people, I carry pepper spray now," said Dunn. In fact, two years after the attack, Dunn encountered another bear while running on the Teton Crest Trail near Grand Teton National Park. This time, however, he was running with three friends, all women, and the bear was a black bear.

"We weren't twenty yards from this bear and I'm standing there looking at him and just feeling so vulnerable, like I just wanted to dig a hole and just go hide somewhere," said Dunn. "And it was really great because these three women I was with kind of pushed me to the back and just said, 'Don't worry about it, we'll take care of it.' They just started saying, 'Hey bear, hey bear, you know we're just people' and this bear looked at us and just sort of took off. So I'm just doing the right thing in terms of safety in bear country, definitely wiser about that."

Since that attack, Dunn has also been in demand as a motivational speaker, attending conferences as far away as Australia and speaking to audiences as varied as trucking unions and church groups. He talks about the importance of following rules, "I was definitely not in compliance with the rules in terms of what you should be doing in bear country that day." He talks about relying on instinct, "there were a lot of things that I did that day that got me into trouble but there were also a lot of things that I followed that day that probably saved my life." Lastly, and most importantly, he talks about overcoming obstacles, "I think there are a lot of people who in my situation, kind of get in that victim mentality. They are like 'Well, I've been attacked by a bear and woe is me.' I just felt so lucky, so blessed, that I have got to make something of my life so I took on a lot of things.

"The other thing is, ironically enough, instead of making me more passive about doing those kinds of things, it's actually emboldened me in a lot of ways," said Dunn. "There's still some aspects of being in bear country that I don't totally enjoy and I'm not totally comfortable even camping now but I'm getting more and more used to it."

As for the bear, park officials did not pursue it. Much of the reasoning was that the bear was surprised by Dunn, was in a remote area, and had no prior history with humans. Some officials speculated the bear was a female with cubs and she had been staring at her cubs in the woods. Park rangers visited Dunn in the hospital shortly after the attack. "They said, 'Well do you want us to go after this bear, are you comfortable with that?'

"I didn't even have to think about it," said Dunn. "It was not like I'm some real big naturalist or conservationist, but I didn't even have to think about it, I just said, 'No, absolutely not.' I think the reason why was I knew immediately that this was not a malicious attack by this bear. There's a real misconception that people have that bears are like muggers sort of waiting for people and are predatory like that. Nothing could be further from the truth. And so what I said, was 'Hey, I was on the bear's turf, this is not a question of needing to go get the bear, I was on the bear's turf. So no, do not go after this bear.'

"I know that not only shocked some people, it actually upset some other people who . . . unfortunately there's still kind of a western mentality of 'Circle the wagons, let's go get the posse and go get this guy.' And if anything—here's the weird thing— I felt really, really, blessed that I was even alive. I mean the bear could have killed me at any instant, just snapped my neck. I had not even an ounce of ill feeling towards this bear. And I think they definitely have their place and need their spaces. It's not that there are more bear attacks in Wyoming because the bears are coming more into people's places, it's because we're building more places in Wyoming that are right in bear habitat.

"So what I think what it does is that it teaches you the preciousness of life," said Dunn. "You look at every day like, 'Wow, every day is a really, really special day.' Even when I had bad days—not to say that every day is great and that I never have bad days—but I think your perspective changes a little bit. You know that you are really glad to be here."

Cool heads, hot summer

*Two hikers in Yellowstone make a good team to survive a
bear attack*

Tom Crosson didn't like the look on his buddy's face. Nils
Wygant was about to run. If he ran, they were in trouble. Trouble
was, Crosson himself was running.

"As I was running, I saw his face and I could tell that he was
about to follow my example," said Crosson, "and I think it was
the look on his face and realizing that he was about to run, was
what made me realize what I was doing was so stupid. So I
yelled 'Don't run!' and I hit the deck."

Behind him, charging "like a train" up the stream bank and
closing fast was a female grizzly with three cubs. She was angry
and she was almost on top of him before he could turn and
move. But when Crosson flopped belly-down on the forest floor,
the bear slammed to a stop, back feet sliding, front legs out-
stretched like a good calf-roping horse at Cheyenne Frontier
Days. For a split second, it appeared as if an attack had been
avoided, and if the two men just played dead they would be
okay.

Tom Crosson and Nils Wygant were outdoors buddies, men
drawn to nature for its beauty and solace. For the New En-
glanders—Crosson, a veterinarian from Massachusetts, and
Wygant, a computer programmer from New Hampshire—this
trip to Yellowstone National Park was the pinnacle of the outdoors experience.

This was Crosson's fifth trip to Yellowstone, and after each previous trip, he'd tell Wygant about the wonders of the nation's first national park and beg him to go on the next trip. Finally, after consulting with his wife and children, Wygant decided he'd go "Out West."

On September 2, 2002, deep in the Yellowstone backcountry, Crosson and Wygant were finally walking the park's thick forests and enjoying some of the wildest country left in the Lower Forty-Eight. The day before they'd taken a boat taxi across the broad sweep of Yellowstone Lake to a landing called Columbine Point, where Columbine Creek enters the lake. After getting dropped off and hanging a large duffle bag of spare gear from a pole that was out of reach of bears, they backpacked down the shore about three miles to a campsite on the lake. There they set up a base camp from which they planned to take day hikes and stay the next several nights. Both men were excited to be in the park and they were prepared for almost anything.

Planning for this trip had been top-to-bottom, and at the very top of the list of things to buy when they arrived in Yellowstone was pepper spray, also known as capsicum spray. Using cayenne pepper extract as its active ingredient, pepper spray is fast emerging as the prudent backcountry traveler's friend and is widely considered to be more effective than a firearm in stopping bear attacks. It is manufactured by a number of companies and is worn in a hip or shoulder holster for quick action. A plastic "safety" on the can prevents accidental spraying and the safety can be quickly thumbed off during a bear charge.

A canister of pepper spray is no larger than the average can of aerosol deodorant and works on much the same principle. A propellant shoots the active ingredient—in this case, oleoresin capsicum—into the air in a cone-shaped shotgun-blast pattern with an effective range of twenty-five feet or less. In essence it is bear mace. A human coming into contact with even a little bit of pepper spray will find himself writhing on the ground half-blind, eyes watering, throat constricting, choking, and wanting to vomit. It's rough stuff, and it's highly effective. Bear-attack expert and researcher Stephen Herrero, author of *Bear Attacks: Their Causes and Avoidance*, conducted a study of its actual use. Herrero found that pepper spray was effective in fifteen out of sixteen cases where grizzly or Alaskan brown bears were acting aggressively.

Crosson and Wygant had each gotten a canister of pepper spray when they arrived in the park. "It was kind of the rule that we talked about all along," said Wygant. "It was the first item on the agenda. Get that stuff, put it on your belt, and then take it off when the trip's over. And that's what we did. Once we went through the motions of buying it and putting it on your hip and having it there for the first couple of hours and later on that day, I kind of forgot about it."

The first two days of their trip had been spent playing tourist in Yellowstone, driving around the park and visiting the various attractions. The men wore their cans of pepper spray everywhere. "Even when we were going through volcano-this and mudflat-that," said Wygant, "It was always there."

That first evening in the backcountry, they realized they had left a bottle of schnapps with the extra gear at Columbine Point. It sure would be nice to have a little something to nip on around the campfire. So the next morning they planned a trip back to Columbine Point. They could just hike down the trail three miles, but they wanted to see some of the country. Why not make a loop hike?

They decided to hike up a dry creek bed that cut deep into the hills east of the lake. By looking on the map and using a GPS, they found a place where the dry creek came close to Columbine Creek. At that point, they would climb out of the dry creek, cross over to Columbine Creek, and go down it to Columbine Point. They would retrieve the schnapps and then take the trail back to base camp. It would be a perfect loop on a perfect day. Indeed, the day was already remarkable. Crosson, an avid bird watcher, had added a black-backed woodpecker to his life list.

At a point where the dry creek bed got very close to Columbine Creek, the men scrambled up the bank onto the small ridge between the two creeks. They thought this would be a good place to stop for a snack and water. Crosson took off his fanny pack and stepped over to look down at Columbine Creek. What happened next happened fast.

"I hear this crashing and I'm not really sure what's going on at first," said Crosson, "I look down and it's a mother grizzly with cubs and she had one on each side and at that time I couldn't see the third, but apparently there was one in back of her and they were tearing through the woods and she was probably about thirty feet away from me when I first saw her and she was coming at me like a locomotive. She was just coming all out and the ground is all flying in the air around them. They are coming fast. Coming through the brush. The best image I have of the bear is of that head breaking through the brush and then all of this stuff kicking up like a four-wheeler trying to get up a leaf-covered hill and everything just flying into the air."

The sow's ears were lying flat on her head and she was in a full-steam charge. As she ran, she made a low guttural grunt with each lunge. It was "hurrrumpf, hurrrumpf, hurrrumpf, hurrrumpf," a sound that was half-growl, half-forced exhale, and all frightening. Dirt flying, a virtual herd of bears coming at him, and that sound: it's little wonder that Crosson's first instinct was to run.

"I turned and I stupidly ran like three steps back to Nils," said Crosson. The men were only about ten feet apart. "As I was running I am yelling, 'We've got a grizzly, she's coming fast, she's got cubs! Don't run!'"

Then Crosson threw himself face down in the dirt and pulled his fanny pack up over his neck. Although Crosson's first instinct had been to run, his common sense and training had taken over. The bear slid to a halt.

Wygant's first instinct was to pull his bear spray in a fluid quick-draw. "I was doing my back-peddling and I was also reaching for the bear spray and I had that out of the holster and in my hand when I hit the deck. I don't know where the reflex came from but when I was down . . . the spray was in my hand."

Now with both men lying parallel on the ground and Crosson closest to the sow, she hesitated for a tick, almost as if deciding the next step. Although Crosson had his face in the dirt, Wygant, only five feet away, kept watching the bear.

"When I hit the deck I did not bury my face, I kept my head up and, keeping my eye on her, I kind of tracked her," said Wygant. "Tom was in her direct charge but because I never took my eyes off of her, I have this movie in my head of this whole thing and she did the classic grizzly bear bluff charge. She completely halted her charge. She definitely bluffed and then decided, 'No, I'm going to go through with this,' and then she exploded on him."

The bear chomped down on Crosson's left leg below the knee. "You know how a big dog would take a rope and play tug of war? You know how they sort of whip themselves to yank it? That was it," said Wygant, "and it's a 400-plus pound animal doing that."

The force of the bite and the shake lifted Crosson's lower body off the ground. "I let out like a one note yell," said Crosson. "I screamed but I think my brain was saying I shouldn't be screaming, so I just let out one AWWWW!"

Wygant was so close he could have reached out and touched the bear. It was too much for him to lie there and watch. "(She) gave him a good bite and then a shake and he screams out in this . . . it was a weird kind of 'Aaaah!' because it was clear that he was trying to stifle it with the whole play-dead thing but it was also clear that he was scared to death and, and, in great pain. It was all those things mixed into that one sound. I'll never forget it."

It was enough to bring Wygant back up to his knees, holding his bear spray. His movement broke the sow's concentration. She looked up, turned toward her cubs which were milling and whimpering about ten feet off the men's heads, jumped toward them to check on them, then spun and went for Wygant. In a millisecond Wygant dropped back down on his stomach with his bear spray propped up before him combat-style, "kind of like an Army guy prone in the desert with his gun."

At some point, whether it was when he first pulled the spray from its holster or when he rose to his knees, Wygant took the safety off the can and was ready to fire. But he waited until he knew he had a can't-miss shot.

"I hesitated just a half a second," said Wygant. He wanted to make the first shot of spray the best shot. Later he admitted he could have sprayed her at almost any moment previously, but there wasn't a good angle and he wasn't sure of the range. So he waited. "I waited until she exploded at me and she got about halfway, about five feet, and I sprayed."

The spray shot out of the can like it was coming out of a fire extinguisher, and a cone-shaped red cloud hit the sow grizzly full in the face.

"She came to a complete stop five feet away and gave like a little whaaaaafffff," said Wygant. "I mean she went from everything she's got to nothing in five feet. For a ten-foot explosive charge, you can pretty much figure that you are going to get it, but she came to a complete stop at half of that distance, at five feet. All that speed and all that mass and she was able to just completely stop. There was no slow down, it was just boom."

The sow spun ninety degrees and thundered down the dry creek bed that Wygant and Crosson had hiked up, her three cubs running after her.

Although Crosson was injured, he was concentrating on playing dead, his face still down in the dirt, the fanny pack still wrapped around his neck. "All I can remember thinking was, 'What should I be doing now?'" said Crosson. "A second later, 'What should I be doing now?' And it was just continually reevaluating that decision. Then hearing the pepper spray go off but not knowing what it was at the time and it sounded like a fire extinguisher being released.

"The next thing I remember is hearing Nils say, 'I got her! Tom! I got her good!' And that's what brought my head up."

The bear and her cubs were gone. Wygant stood up and looked at his buddy and immediately his eyes flicked to Crosson's lower left leg. Crosson's hiking pants were torn and there was blood pooling below his knee.

"I saw his leg and then reality, as if it's not real enough already, reality really starts to sink in," said Wygant. "I realized how screwed we were."

They were miles from help. They didn't have a cell phone and cell phones are useless anyway that deep in the backcountry. Rescue facilities were all the way on the other side of Wyoming's largest lake.

In fact, the two were better off than most people would have been in that situation. Wygant had first aid experience and had actually taken an emergency medical technician course many years before. Better yet, Crosson was a doctor—a veterinarian—but a doctor nevertheless. He also had EMT training.

While Crosson stayed face down in the duff, Wygant went to work, pulling out a knife and cutting Crosson's pants so he could tend to the wound. Wygant pulled off his own shirt and dug into his daypack for an extra pair of wind pants. The bear had bitten deeply into Crosson's leg, leaving two long gashes. The pressure of the bite had also broken the fibula, the smaller of the two bones in the lower leg. Although they didn't know it at the time, the bite had also severely damaged the peroneal nerve in Crosson's leg, which made him unable to bend his foot at the ankle when he walked.

Wygant did a quick cleaning of the six- or seven-inch gashes and then wrapped his shirt and pants around his friend's leg. Meanwhile, Crosson directed Wygant in the vagaries of pressure-wrapping a wound—too tight and it becomes a tourniquet, too loose and it's ineffective. Then Wygant, still displaying a cool head, dug into his pack and pulled out his camera. He took a picture. At the time, Crosson was thinking, "Let's get the hell out of here, but actually in hindsight, I'm very glad he did that."

Wygant rose to his feet and looked around. They could go back down the dry creek bed. It was easy walking, a virtual highway back to their campsite. Or they could bushwhack down Columbine Creek and come out at Columbine Point like they had planned. The day before, a group of doctors had also been dropped off at the point. Maybe if they were lucky, the doctors or somebody would still be there. But more important and paramount in their decision-making, the sow and her cubs had run down the dry creek bed. They had enough of her. There was no way they wanted to get near her again. So with one of Crosson's arms gripping Wygant's shoulder and with bear spray drawn and ready, they half-hopped, half-plunged down into Columbine Creek.

It was torturous going. "I would say the walk back to Columbine Point was almost as exciting as the attack," said Crosson. "We'd have to get out and climb over dead timber that would be multiple trunks high, and we were on our bellies climbing over deadwood, under deadwood. It was real rough. We both have our pepper sprays out, safeties off, and making sure we aren't spraying each other, waiting for the bear to return. We are blowing our whistles, I'm screaming my head off and hoping we'd get someone's attention walking down the Thorofare Trail, but obviously we're in the middle of nowhere."

They had to wade into the creek to go around logjams. Then they had to climb out of the creek to avoid deep pools. They had to climb over deadfall ten or more feet tall. Wygant would climb out of the serpentine creek bed to look over the bank for a better route, then return to help his friend to the next bend in the creek. It was a process they repeated again and again.

"My leg's broken and my foot's dropped," said Crosson. "I couldn't understand at the time why I kept tripping over my toes. It's just that I didn't have the ability to pick my toes up. It was probably three miles back to Columbine Point and we were now completely off trail and very happy to have a GPS." Crosson's leg started to bleed again and the blood quickly pooled in his boot.

Eventually they reached Columbine Point. There was nobody within miles. That realization was devastating. They'd been attacked, they'd bushwhacked for hours down a remote mountain stream, and they saw the lake as salvation. But there was no rescue to be had.

"That was my first emotional shot when we got back to Columbine Point and nobody was there," said Crosson. "That's when the tears started to run, not because of the pain, but I was really depending upon somebody being there and there wasn't."

But neither man lost his cool. The attack had happened mid-morning and the bushwhack down the creek had eaten up the day. Now, as the sun slowly arched to the west over the broad back of Yellowstone Lake, they realized they'd have to spend the night there. And, through luck or good planning, they were prepared for doing just that.

The duffle bag they had left at the point wasn't just any duffle bag. It was filled with all kinds of backup gear. In fact, although Crosson remembers getting some grief for bringing so much extra gear to cache, it would be the men's deliverance. Inside the duffle was an extra sleeping bag, an extra air mattress, food, an extra stove, bottled water, and—best of all—the mother of all first aid kits. Crosson had drawn on his veterinary expertise and had raided his clinic for a number of items that aren't in most first aid kits. He'd packed gauze, several different antibiotics, assorted swabs and ointments, and a breathable wrap commonly called vet wrap.

"We never lost our ability to think straight," said Crosson. "We counted our blessings that we had hung this massive pack of extra gear. We had a lot of equipment."

Now they could properly take care of the wounds. While Crosson directed his own first aid, Wygant flushed the wounds with the bottled water and swabbed on ointments, then wrapped the whole works with the vet wrap.

Even though Crosson was afraid that he'd slip into shock and Wygant was operating on overload, the medical care was first rate. While Wygant took notes, Crosson figured out the proper dosage of antibiotics for his body weight. Wygant wrote down the calculations, the time and amount of dosage, and his friend's vital signs.

It was now late in the day and there was a chill wind coming off the lake. Wygant went into what he called "firewood gathering mode," preparing for the night ahead. While

Wygant was collecting wood, Crosson was thinking of the next step.

"He's still clear minded and that immobility gave him all the time in the world to think of ideas, think of good things, kind of keep me busy," said Wygant. "So while I'm out there collecting tons and tons of firewood, he's one step ahead of me thinking about shelter and what might be some good ideas for shelter so between the two of us, his ideas and my running around, we slung together this wind-breaker kind of shelter."

They were lakeside at an old campsite that had been closed to rehabilitate the vegetation. But the old campsite still had a fire-ring and was surrounded by large logs for sitting. Wygant stacked those logs into a triangular shape, two logs high with an open end to the fire. Then he put a plastic bag over the top of the logs and was able to get his friend inside. As darkness fell, Wygant stoked the fire and prepared for an all-night vigil.

About a mile and a half away across the Southeast Arm of Yellowstone Lake rises a peninsula of land called The Promontory. Backcountry campsites are also along its shoreline. Perhaps someone over there might help them, so when Wygant rose during the night to build up the fire, he tried signaling for help. Wygant flashed an S.O.S. with his headlamp. He blew three short blasts on his whistle, a universal backcountry distress signal. He fed the fire into a roaring blaze. This process was repeated every twenty minutes throughout the night.

When one thirty in the morning rolled around, he remembered being relieved because daylight was finally going to come. He was exhausted. Late in the night, a bull elk started bugling far off and then came closer. Wygant remembers thinking, "Just go away." He'd had his fill of nature. By dawn, he was completely drained, emotionally and physically. His friend was still bleeding occasionally. Crosson's leg was swelling and he was in great pain.

Wygant decided to cover all possibilities for rescue. Some 150 yards behind their camp ran the Thorofare Trail, an oft-traveled backcountry route. On his blaze orange fanny pack he wrote the words "HELP, BEAR ATTACK," filled it with gravel, and placed it right across the trail. If someone was hiking or riding by, they'd see it.

With dawn came activity on the lake. Crosson and Wygant both had binoculars and they watched boats skimming across the water. The campsite itself was marked with a blaze orange triangle set atop a metal post; it can be seen from the water when boats are dropping off backcountry travelers. Wygant dug the post and its triangle out of the ground and waved it at passing boats. They kept passing. No one saw them. No one. It seemed as if they were trapped on the shore.

Wygant ran up and down the beach waving the orange marker in the air, shouting at the top of his lungs, and blowing on the whistle. But the boats kept passing. Wygant and Crosson watched in frustration as a boat rounded The Promontory, landed, and unloaded kayakers and canoers. Although it was only a mile and a half away and it was a bright calm morning, no amount of whistle blowing or shouting could get their attention. They watched as the canoers and kayakers loaded up their gear and started paddling south along The Promontory's shoreline.

"I couldn't believe they couldn't hear us," said Crosson, "and to watch that boat come in and then go away, there's the second breakdown of me emotionally. It was just devastating, and then we watched the people they had dropped off get into canoes and go along the peninsula and we are like, 'Help!!!!!' And we just couldn't get anybody's attention."

A plane flew over and the men lit a signal smoke flare they had with them. The plane didn't see the smoke. Their level of disappointment rose. Both were near tears when they looked up to see a boat heading straight towards them.

Aboard the boat was park wildlife biologist Tiffany Potter, who was studying the presence and distribution of the park's population of the rare Canada lynx. She and an assistant were being dropped off for a five-day backcountry trip to check bait stations and collect hair samples. Potter was concentrating on the day ahead. Ironically, before boarding the boat that morning, Potter had talked to her crew about the need to be extremely cautious because of recent bear activity. That summer there had been several incidents between humans and bears, and a vital bear food, the whitebark pine, which produces a high-energy nut, was coming off a very poor year.

"(I was saying) bears have been coming down lower seeking alternative foods into places where there's a lot of people," remembered Potter. "We really need to be on high alert."

The boat slowed and came to shore, and Potter and her crew got ready to disembark. They didn't even see Wygant, despite all of his running and shouting and orange-marker waving, until he reached the boat.

"I grabbed hold of the bow," said Wygant. "It was another of those moments of salvation, one of those really clear memories. And my hands held on, I held on tight."

"Nils grabbed the boat and he was crying," said Potter, "and he could just barely squeeze out the words, 'We barely survived the night. My friend was mauled by a bear.' It was just one of those moments you'll never forget."

Potter came ashore and noticed the camp. It looked like a shanty camp with the plastic tarp and makeshift shelter. She noticed Crosson sitting with his back to the shore. As she walked up, she didn't know what to expect. From the rear, she could see that his pant legs were soaked in blood. "And his leg was kind of tucked up underneath a log," said Potter. "From the back it looked like he had no leg, so I was thinking to myself, 'This man has a nub. He has a stump. This is way out of my league.'"

With great relief she discovered that Crosson was not missing limbs. She quickly assessed his injuries and decided to leave the bandaging on his leg because she didn't want to start the bleeding all over again. Her crew got the men's gear ready for rescue. A rescue boat was called and it quickly arrived. To Crosson, it was an amazing event.

"It was like the entire park just threw down whatever they were doing at the time and ran to my aid. I can't say enough about the park service, they were just absolutely wonderful," said Crosson.

As the story unfolded, Potter found herself impressed by the men. "The two of them were really, really well prepared," said Potter. "It seems as if the stories that I read about bear mauling victims is that they seem relatively inexperienced. What was neat about this whole situation is that they had first aid equipment, they had an extra set of stuff on the shore so if there was an emergency away from their camp, and Tom was so coherent and knew exactly what was going on with his system."

Potter went with Wygant and Crosson across the lake to Bridge Bay Marina where an ambulance was waiting. Potter's crew boated three miles down the shore and took down Wygant and Crosson's backcountry camp.

As soon as the men boarded the rescue boat, their entire attitude shifted. They were rescued. They were safe. It was over.

At Lake Hospital in Yellowstone, Crosson was treated for his injuries. It was twenty-two hours after the attack and doctors found his wounds were sterile. The antibiotics and emergency medical care had been top notch.

Word of the attack spread quickly. Wygant and Crosson were interviewed by the news media and even appeared on NBC's

"Today Show." The *Boston Globe* featured the attack, and when they arrived back home in the Boston airport several days later, a camera crew from FOX television greeted them at the baggage claim. Several months later, New Hampshire Governor Craig Benson presented Wygant with a hero's award.

Crosson reveled in the spotlight. "I love the attention to be honest with you," he said. "My big joke is I'll do anything for attention including getting attacked by a grizzly bear. Everybody is in awe, it just makes such a great story. Now if I had fallen off a cliff and broken my back and had real medical problems, I don't think I would have gotten as much attention as being attacked by a grizzly."

Crosson had been living in an apartment next to his clinic in Springfield, Massachusetts. Not long after the attack, he bought a cabin in the Berkshire Mountains surrounded by acres and acres of deep woods. "Christ, I just got attacked by a grizzly bear," Crosson told himself. "How long are you going to wait before you spend money, you going to die wealthy?"

Wygant has little desire to go back into the Yellowstone backcountry, but the same is not true for the enthusiastic Crosson. Several surgeries after the attack, he still has only marginal control over his foot because of the nerve damage. He has to wear a brace, but "the brace fits into a hiking boot," said Crosson. "I can't wait to get back. I can't wait to get back into the backcountry, I can't wait to go back and try to find the spot where I got attacked. The problem is none of my friends' wives will let them go. I will have many more trips to Yellowstone."

It will probably be next to impossible to convince Wygant to go with him. "I guess I can see the value in that, but can't imagine the circumstances when I'd be comfortable doing that," said Wygant. He is comfortable hiking in his New England mountains, only now he packs bear spray with him when he goes.

"I would say to anybody, even if you are a hunter, have it because I just can't imagine in that scenario, I just can't imagine getting a shot off, let alone being a shot that works," said Wygant. "Most of the people I talk to say, 'Oh, I would have had this gun or I would have had that gun,' and first they don't realize you can't have a gun in Yellowstone but second of all I'm glad I had the spray rather than the gun. I mean you are going to miss him (with a gun). You are going to miss or you are going to make him angry."

As for the bear, "I think that I ran into a really good mother," said Crosson. "She was doing her job and she did it well and I'm very thankful that she didn't kill me and I have no bad feelings toward her at all. We certainly knew that this was bear territory and we were taking some risk. Now the statistics were in our favor, but as they say if the statistics are one in a million, but if it happens to you, it happens to you 100 percent."

The incident came near the end of an unusual summer. Wyoming wilted under the third straight year of drought. While the high plateau that makes up most of Yellowstone National Park wasn't hit as hard as the state's low sagebrush basins, the park nevertheless was not immune to the crispy conditions. Drought certainly could have brought grizzly bears down into the lower lodgepole expanse from high plateaus. A poor whitebark pine year didn't help. Other bear food sources were meager too. Whatever the cause, the park did have a higher than normal number of bear incidents in 2002. Yet in almost every case, cool heads ruled the day.

No one's head was cooler than that of Abigail Thomas, who was working a summer postal service job at Lake Village. On Sunday, May 26, Thomas went for an early morning run around the tourist cabins at Lake. As she rounded a bend, she encountered a young grizzly bear in a parking lot. She stopped running as the bear stood up on its hind legs, then dropped down and started ambling toward her.

Thomas stood as quietly as she could. She'd only been in the park about three weeks, but she'd absorbed some of the tips for encounters with grizzlies—don't run, avoid eye contact, try to be non-threatening, and carry bear spray. Unfortunately, she didn't have any bear spray, only a water bottle.

She told the *Bozeman* (Montana) *Daily Chronicle* that she talked in a low tone of voice, saying "Hey bear, leave me alone." Still the bear walked right up to her and started sniffing her. Then it opened its mouth and took her right thigh in its jaws. Thomas didn't run. She didn't panic. She shouted, "Go away bear!"

The bear let go of her thigh but it didn't leave. At one time in her life Thomas had pulled a stint as a veterinary technician at an animal hospital. She'd dealt with aggressive dogs, but this bear seemed more curious than anything. So she aimed her water bottle at the bear and gave it a squeeze, dousing it right between the eyes.

"He seemed kind of startled by that," she told the newspaper. The bear backed off and ambled slowly away.

The bear's bite hadn't even broken the skin. It did cause some bruising, but the incident didn't keep Thomas from continuing to run that summer. But she vowed to carry her bear spray, which she had forgotten that morning. She, like Crosson, got a hefty dose of media attention, appearing on ABC's "Good Morning America" and later on LifetimeTV's program called "What Should You Do."

In most years, Yellowstone only averages one human injury from bears (both black and grizzly), which is vastly different from the forty-eight per year that the park averaged from the 1930s to the 1960s. While most of those early-day incidents were bear-teasing tourists getting slapped or nipped by annoyed black bears, it does look as if the park's longtime, intensive effort to educate people is working. "We've got a real big program of preventative management and education," said Yellowstone bear management biologist Kerry Gunther. "We put a lot into the front end to let people know about grizzly bears."

Even more remarkable is the fact that Yellowstone receives more than three million visitors each year now and bear numbers seem to be on the rise as well. "It used to be fairly rare to see bears, now we're seeing them all the time," said Gunther.

Yellowstone is still a very wild place, despite all of the visitors. By far the bulk of the park's visitors never get very far off the main roads and those who camp out in the backcountry only log about 45,000 user nights per year. Away from the roads, the deep backcountry is pristine, wild, relatively untouched. Bear country.

Bear in the bedroom

Wyoming black bears in and out of houses, trees, traps, and trucks

It gets hot in the middle of summer in the high desert turned farm country that surrounds Riverton, Wyoming. On summer nights, folks sleep with their windows and patio doors open and hardly any covers on their beds.

It is a country of sugar beets and antelope, with the forested shoulders of the Wind River Range on the far horizon and a sea of sagebrush between. It's anything but bear country, and that's why RoJean Thayer was thinking anything but bear when something brushed her leg in the middle of a June night in 1994. In that blurry state between consciousness and sleep, she thought the neighbor's dog had somehow gotten into the house. She woke up her husband, Terry.

"I woke up and I smelled, you know how a dog smells when its wet?" Terry remembered. "I had that smell and I saw a shadow of something in the bedroom and I immediately, because of the smell, assumed it was the neighbor's dog. So I just hopped out of bed and said 'Shoo, get out of here!' and as soon as I said something, it started taking off, like it knew where it was supposed to go."

In the dim light, the animal looked like a dog, but as Terry chased it out of the bedroom into the living room and out the open sliding glass door, it paused. It was then that Terry thought something wasn't quite right. But the animal left and Terry went back to bed, still cursing the neighbor's dog for getting into their house.

A few hours later, still in the thick of the night, "our daughter busted into the house and said there was a bear in her yard," Terry said. Then it clicked: the "dog" in their house hadn't been a dog after all. "We jumped into the pickup and ran over there and sure enough, there was a bear at the base of this tree."

The Thayers went back to their house and called the Fremont County Sheriff's Department, which directed them to Chris Daubin, a warden with the Wyoming Game and Fish Department in Riverton.

"I can still remember what RoJean said when she called," said Daubin. "She said, 'There was a bear in our bedroom,' and I asked, 'What are you going to do now?' and she said, 'I'm sure not going back to bed!'"

Since Riverton is so far from the mountains, there's no need for the local game warden to have a bear trap. Daubin had to call the department's district office in Lander and wait for a trap to arrive. Several hours later, Daubin darted the young black bear in a tree, loaded it into the trap, and took it back to the mountains.

Apparently the bear had been spending some time in the neighborhood, eating dog food on porches and rummaging around. Something had gotten into a neighbor's garbage, and the Thayers' daughter had her kitchen trashed by what she assumed was a raccoon.

When Terry sat down and thought about that night, he realized the sliding glass door on their patio had been closed when they went to bed. Upon investigation, he found scratch marks on the door where the bear had opened it.

These days the Thayers still laugh about their bear, and friends have given them carved wooden bears as gag gifts. "I'm sort of glad we found the bear (at the daughter's house) because no one would have believed the story otherwise," said Terry. "To be honest with you, if the circus had been in town, I would have thought maybe that bear had ran away from the circus."

Black bears don't have the nasty reputation that their grizzly cousins do. In fact, people seem to like black bears, perhaps spurred on by Hollywood, Gentle Ben, Smoky Bear, and Yogi Bear. All are black bears. Even though black bears have mauled and killed people, the American public generally sees them as happy-go-lucky and harmless.

Indeed, in Yellowstone National Park, feeding roadside black bears was a popular activity for tourists in the 1910s, '20s and '30s. The bears became so tame they were celebrated in magazine articles and children's books. Some were even given nicknames such as "Spud, The Hold-up Bear of the Yellowstone" and "Jesse James." These habituated bears often sat in the same roadside spot day after day, waiting for handouts. Early photos show tourists and even rangers feeding the bears by hand.

Even today a black bear evokes more curiosity than fear. One reason is that a black bear's natural instinct is to run or climb a tree, while a grizzly will often bluff charge. Black bears are also more common. In Wyoming black bears live almost anywhere there is good bear habitat.

Because they are more widespread and more numerous than grizzly bears, black bears actually have more conflicts with man. When bears have encounters with people outside the national parks, the Wyoming Game and Fish Department gets the call. Often the department's wardens are the employees who respond.

One summer day in 1980, Ron Iverson got that call. At the time, Iverson was a game warden stationed in Lander and tasked with law enforcement and wildlife management on the southeastern flanks of the massive Wind River Range. For several days he had been trying to trap a black bear that was raiding camps around Dickinson Park, a popular recreational area in the mountains north of Lander and just outside Fort Washakie on the Wind River Indian Reservation. The plan was to take the bear far away from Dickinson, down around the southern toe of the mountain range to Pine Creek on the west side of the range, a move of many miles of bad dirt road and good paved highway.

When the call came that there was a bear in the culvert trap, Iverson thought this was a perfect time for a family outing, so he swung by his house and picked up his two young sons and his two dogs. After all, moving a black bear in a live trap from one location to another is a fairly routine procedure.

The trap is the aptly named culvert trap, which is essentially a long, cave-like metal culvert with a heavy metal gate on one end. The trap is baited with road kill or some other bear delicacy, and when the bear climbs into the trap to get the bait, the door slams shut and is locked. The trap is mounted on wheels, complete with trailer hitch and lights. It can be simply hooked onto a truck and pulled to whatever location is necessary. There, the door is pulled open and the bear launches out into new country.

"My boys, Kip, four, and Casey, six, had been with me several times before, but it had been awhile and after about five minutes, I remembered why," said Iverson in an account of his adventure that day. "When they weren't busy fightin' with each other, they were giving me all kinds of technical advice. They seemed to have all the answers, only I don't think they understood the questions."

The road to Dickinson Park is a twisted, rocky number that winds its way up the face of the Wind River foothills. On a good day it's a bad road, with numerous steep switchbacks, lots of sharp, tire-ripping rocks, and blind corners. The road climbs through the desert, onto the sagebrush shoulders, and finally into the lodgepole and aspen highlands of the range. Much of the road is on the reservation, but when it finally levels off, it bends south back into the national forest. Finally it breaks out in the high mountain country with large open parks complete with an idyllic stream or two and tall granite peaks in the distance. One of these peaks is fittingly called Bears Ears and it was here that Iverson and his two sons reached the trap and its contents.

"Everything was going real smooth," said Iverson, "the kids hadn't given me any technical advice and hadn't gotten into a fight since we had pulled up to the trap. The troublemaker, Mr. Bruin, was busy finishing up the bait for breakfast and didn't seem to mind our presence."

Iverson hitched the trap to his pickup truck and started down the mountain, back over that famously ugly road. Iverson decided to release the bear down by South Pass, but to get there, he'd have to drive through the towns of Fort Washakie and Lander with the bear in the trap, the dogs in the bed of the pickup, and the boys riding shotgun.

The trap itself was built without any springs or shocks of any kind, so the trip down was rough. Iverson reasoned that the maker of the trap neglected to put on shocks for a reason. "He didn't want things too comfortable for whatever was riding back there," said Iverson. "I think he did that to make sure those bears were ready to come out when you got to where you was going." This strategy apparently worked. "The bears I released came out of that trap like they were shot out of a cannon," Iverson said.

So they pounded down the mountain over some twenty miles of tortured road, bear bouncing in tow. When Iverson got to Fort Washakie, he noticed an unusual reaction from some of the citizens as he drove by. "The people coming out of the local grocery store had really taken an interest in us. As a matter of fact, they were staring at us like most folks would stare at a whore in church," recounted Iverson. "Christ, there were people dropping grocery sacks, runnin' into one another, and fallin' over things. I guess we were quite a sight."

Meanwhile, the boys had gotten bored with the whole affair and were starting to make a lot of noise. Distracted by the boys, Iverson thought little of the reaction of the people in Fort Washakie and drove out of town into farmland and open country. About two miles out of town, his dogs, a yellow lab named Sundance and a black mutt named Blackie, started barking wildly from the back of the pickup.

Iverson couldn't see into the back of the truck, so he told his oldest boy, Casey, to stand on the seat and see what was going on.

"Dad," came the answer, "the bear's out of the trap."

"The kid being a born practical joker, I said, 'Quit clownin' around and tell me what is going on back there.'" Iverson recalled. Casey insisted the bear was loose.

"I adjusted the rearview mirror and took a look. Holy hell, the kid was right, I could see the tips of the bear's ears above the tailgate of the truck. Someway, somehow, that darn bear had crawled out of the trap and was sitting on the tongue of the trailer. Just getting a little fresh air, I guess." Immediately Iverson knew why people had been acting so strangely in Fort Washakie.

The bear was riding balanced on the trailer tongue while Iverson clipped down the highway at sixty-five miles per hour. "I started slowing down, not really knowing what I was going to do after I got stopped," said Iverson.

When the truck got down to about thirty-five miles per hour, the bear bailed out, hit the pavement, and started spinning all fours down the highway. Then the bear made a beeline for a couple of trailer houses on the side of the highway. Iverson slammed on the brakes, jumped out, released the dogs, grabbed a rope and a duffle bag, and set off in hot pursuit, yelling at his boys to stay in the truck. Since it wasn't a very large bear, Iverson's flash decision was to rope the bear and somehow get it stuffed into the bag.

Meanwhile, the bear, with the dogs in hot pursuit, ran beneath the first house trailer, out the other side, beneath the second house trailer, and through a yard where two small children were playing. As Iverson galloped by in pursuit, he could see the little kids pointing at the bear and yelling for their mother. The bear ran over a little hill and down to the shores of Ray Lake, a large reservoir in the middle of the reservation surrounded by ranchland and widely scattered houses. Without hesitation, the bear hit the water and started swimming, the dogs following. Iverson, out of wind, bent over huffing at the shore.

It was time to regroup. Iverson called his dogs back to him while the bear swam into the middle of the lake, heading for the far shore and the only trees for miles around. Unfortunately, those tall cottonwoods were "right smack in the middle of a farmer's yard."

Iverson walked back to his truck, working out a plan in his head. He called the Fremont County Sheriff's dispatch center, relating that his prisoner had escaped and was swimming across Ray Lake. "Was the search and rescue boat available?" he asked.

Iverson drove around the lake to the farmer's place and waited for the bear to swim a mile or so across. The plan was to keep the bear in the water until the boat arrived, then somehow rope the bear and get it back into the trap. As the bear neared the shore, Iverson released his dogs to try to keep the bruin in the water. The bear had different ideas.

"The bear's thoughts were to get into one of those big ol' eighty-foot cottonwood trees," said Iverson.

Finally the bear got into water shallow enough that it could stand up on its hind feet. Unfortunately for the dogs, they couldn't touch bottom.

The bear "was swatting them dogs as they swam around him," said Iverson. "He'd smack a dog and under it'd go. Soon the dogs were tired and came to shore with the bear behind. So there we all were, me on the bank above the bear, the bear sittin' on the beach lookin' at a dog on each side of him, and the dogs sittin' looking at the bear. Well, everybody kinda got rested up and the bear decided to make his move. He went for the weakest point—me."

The bear bounded up the bank towards Iverson. "I knew I had to do something, so I built a loop with my rope and gave her a toss," he recounted. "I was a bareback bronc rider in college, not a roper. I missed."

But as luck would have it, part of the limp rope wrapped a couple of times around the bear's neck. The bear was loosely snagged at best, not caught. Iverson took off running toward the house with the bear and the dogs all following.

As this crew ran past Iverson's truck, he noticed his two boys, the farmer and his wife, and a couple of their kids all standing and cheering. "You know, I don't know to this day who they were cheering for, me, the bear, or the dogs," said Iverson.

Somehow Iverson was able to lead the bear to a small Russian olive tree rather than one of the giant cottonwoods, and the bear climbed fast into the tree. Meanwhile the farmer arrived with a rope, and together, Iverson and the farmer were able to "head and heel" the bear and get it back into the trap.

"We put him back into the trap and with a little bailing wire, made 'er escape proof," said Iverson.

The farmer said, "The neighbors aren't ever going to believe this."

Iverson said his goodbyes, loaded up his crew, and headed south. If the bear had waited a few more minutes to make its escape from the trap, it would have been loose in downtown

Lander—a much larger town than Fort Washakie—on a summer weekend day with dozens of people strolling sidewalks and shopping in the town's busy stores. The next morning, he took the bear to an isolated area and turned him loose.

"He really didn't know if he wanted to get out of the trap after what had happened the day before," said Iverson. "But he finally sauntered off."

Before a warden becomes a permanent employee, he or she has to do some time as a trainee, learning the ins and outs of the business before being assigned a warden district. Warden trainees are something like rookie football players at a training camp. They have to do all manner of unglamorous duties that are beneath the seasoned veterans, and they are often the brunt of practical jokes. Sometimes, however, the circumstances alone supply enough ammunition for a lifetime of heckling from peers.

In the summer of 1998, warden trainee Brian Nesvik was called into the Lions Camp for the Blind on Casper Mountain, just outside Casper. The camp is located in a heavily wooded and heavily developed recreational area, an area that Nesvik termed "the perfect place for a garbage-gut bear."

When Nesvik got the call, it was one in the morning and raining. He reluctantly roused himself from bed and climbed into the pickup. The director of the camp reported a bear or bears in the garbage just outside the main lodge. Nesvik worked his way around the back of the lodge, carrying a flashlight in one hand and a dart gun in the other. Meanwhile, Wyoming Game and Fish Department warden Mike Choma and biologist Beau Patterson made their way up the mountain.

"While I was waiting for Mike and Beau to arrive, I decided to walk up and down the road behind the camp, thinking I might be able to find the bear's trail in and out," remembered Nesvik. He walked about a half mile down the road in the rainy darkness and then turned back to the camp. "As I approached the camp, I noticed Mike and Beau just pulling in," said Nesvik. He walked within fifty yards of the truck and into the glare of the headlights when a loud, huffing growl launched him about four feet into the air.

"I observed a 800-pound grizzly bear about fifteen feet away, six feet up a tree," said Nesvik. "The bear was huffing at me and very obviously upset with my presence. It later turned out to be a 150-pound female black bear, but it looked that big to me at the time."

Naturally, Mike and Beau thought Nesvik's reaction was hysterical, and they roared with laughter. When everyone calmed down, they put a spotlight on the bear. Using a dart gun, they tried to tranquilize it so they could move her to a new location.

"As the dart sunk into the bear's behind, she decided to go straight up the tree about sixty feet," said Nesvik. The dart came out as the bear went up the tree, but it looked like a pretty good stick.

Unfortunately for Nesvik, the bear appeared to go to sleep in the tree. "As I was the game warden 'trainee,' there was not even a need to ask who was going to climb the rain-soaked lodgepole to lower the bear to the ground," said Nesvik. "It was raining and the tree was all wet and it was kind of miserable. The bear kind of quit moving around and we thought she had just got hung up in the tree. I thought I'd go up there and either put a rope on her and lower her down or just knock her out of the tree."

It was tough climbing. The tree had few branches and was slick. Nesvik half shimmied, half climbed up the tree, precariously perching on thin, slippery branches, hugging the wet bark.

"After about forty-five minutes, I made it to about three feet below the sleeping bear," said Nesvik. "As I reached for a limb just below the bear, she suddenly growled and huffed at me."

Startled, Nesvik slid down the tree as fast as he could. As he descended, trying not to fall, it started to rain again. But this rain was hot. "It was the bear's way of rudely telling me to leave," said Nesvik. "She just pissed all over my head. The tree that took me forty-five minutes to climb up took me about ten seconds to climb down."

This had Nesvik's audience practically rolling on the ground laughing, while Nesvik was still "scared out of my wits. As I regained my composure, I soon discovered that I was covered with the most foul-smelling fluid Mother Nature had ever allowed to come in contact with my olfactory senses."

When his partners finally regained their composure, they decided to sink another dart into the bear's hide. Then they were able to get the bear out of the tree and into a culvert trap for a 150-mile ride to another home. But on the way they stopped off at Nesvik's home so he could change clothes.

"Beau refused to ride to the south end of Laramie Peak with a bear-urine-smelling game warden trainee," said Nesvik. "I still stunk. It was rotten stuff."

The cabin buster

All was well until someone forgot to latch a door

For thirteen years, the big male bear had been a get-along bear, one of those seldom-seen grizzlies that prowl the Yellowstone country without incident. Bears can live as long as a well-kept horse, fifteen, twenty, even twenty-five years, but in the wild, facing the general hazards of nature such as other grizzlies and the various pitfalls associated with mountain living, thirteen years for a grizzly bear is getting up there. And in an ecosystem filled with livestock and elk hunters, sloppy backcountry campers and unoccupied cabins, a dozen years of anonymity is even more impressive.

All too often, it is human error that gets bears into trouble: dog food left on a porch, bird feeders hung within reach, hotdogs forgotten on a cold barbecue grill, bacon grease poured on the ground in a backcountry hunting camp. A bear has a better memory for a free meal than your worst freeloading, shirttail relative. He'll show up time and again in the same place, and he'll perfect a technique to fill his belly. Bears do not ignore slip-ups and mental burps; it only takes one such lapse in bear country to ruin your outdoor experience and perhaps destroy a bear's life. As wildlife officials often say, a fed bear is a dead bear.

"They are very smart when conditioned relative to food," said Dr. Charles Robbins, director of the Bear Research, Education and Conservation Program at Washington State University in Pullman. Robbins heads the only program of its kind in the world, a facility dedicated solely to captive grizzly bear research. Some bears are permanent residents at Pullman. Four adult bears that were orphaned as cubs are kept on site, which has a two-acre exercise yard and six indoor-outdoor pens with temperature-controlled dens. Researchers and students can study just about every aspect of grizzly life in the facility from hibernation to feeding habits.

"Their life revolves around finding enough food," said Robbins. "So they have plenty of neural circuits for remembering the location of different food resources at different times of the year. After bottle-raising a lot of bears, I consider them just one step below a chimp (in intelligence)."

This impressive brain was clicking right along when the big boar made his way into the Greybull River drainage deep in the backcountry west of the tiny town of Meeteetse, Wyoming. It was late summer 1992. Perhaps he'd spent his entire life in the drainage, but more likely, he was a big grizzly on the move. All grizzlies need big country, but especially males. They wander over 200 to 500 square miles in a lifetime or even a summer. Northwestern Wyoming is the last of the big stuff, and the Greybull is some of the finest even though it is on the far southeastern edge of the wildest country. Beyond and east, the timber thins out into sagebrush and grasslands, irrigated pastures and people.

Most summers, the Greybull country is empty of people. The fishing is marginal and much of the highest country is untrammeled by livestock and cowboys because of the costs of operating in such remote country. But in late summer and fall, it starts to fill up with hunters, particularly sheep hunters for the Greybull is classic bighorn sheep country—rugged tall stuff that brings to mind the bare tundra of Alaska's Brooks Range rather than somewhere in Wyoming's Absarokas.

Even though the drainage is within striking distance for a wandering Yellowstone bear, no one in the Greybull in 1992 was thinking grizzly. The country had been pretty much swiped clean of bears by generations of bear hunters and bear haters. Few people were following "bear camping" methods in that country. But even with the sloppy hunting camps, the big male might have kept out of trouble if it hadn't been for one bonehead move on the part of a human. If someone had just locked the door to the Venus Creek patrol cabin, the big male might have stayed out of trouble, might have kept his anonymity for the rest of his wild life, might have lived a long and successful career as a grizzly bear in country peppered with humans.

The Venus Creek patrol cabin is in an idyllic setting. It's eight miles of easy riding from the trailhead on the Greybull River, tucked back against a stand on lodgepole. Venus Creek flows out of the mountains and past the cabin on its way to join the river. For fifty or more years, backcountry travelers have enjoyed the long views from the cabin's front porch. Most are wilderness rangers or trail crews working for the U.S. Forest Service, but the federal government also allows the employees of other agencies such as the Wyoming Game and Fish Department to enjoy the cabin's convenient location as a base camp for horseback patrols.

A week or so before the big male grizzly ambled up onto the porch and swung open the cabin door, Wyoming game warden Jerry Longobardi had packed in some provisions in anticipation of the upcoming sheep-hunting season. Although he, too, hadn't expected a grizzly bear in that country, Longobardi is a veteran of the backcountry and he'd taken a few precautions. Plus he'd seen some fresh bear scat and he wasn't going to take any chances with his food. He hung it up in the trees, and he stashed a twelve-pack of beer in an empty feed sack, added some rocks, and sunk it deep in the creek. It was a quick in-and-out trip to cache supplies. A Forest Service crew was scheduled to use the cabin before he returned, so he made sure everything was in order and that his own provisions were out of the way.

A couple of weeks later, Longobardi and fellow warden Joe Gilbert rode right past the Venus Creek cabin and deep into the Washakie Wilderness, all the way back into Needle Creek, some of the roughest country in the territory. After a week of scrambling up and down mountains at 12,000 feet, Longobardi and Gilbert decided to ride down to the cabin to resupply.

When they rounded a bend in the trail and saw the Venus Creek cabin in the distance, they knew immediately something was wrong. "We get about 100 yards away and holy smokes, the door was wide open and it looked like somebody had dropped the Pillsbury flour factory in there," said Longobardi.

The destruction was colossal, as if a mini-Midwest tornado had touched down in Wyoming's Greybull River country with precision accuracy focused just on the Venus Creek cabin. Canned goods were strewn everywhere. Pancake mix, flour, pasta, macaroni noodles, dried soup mix, cocoa, coffee, white gasoline containers, tea bags . . . a huge treasure trove of backcountry supplies was scattered helter-skelter.

"For a million years when people stayed at the Venus Cabin they had always left their food and that bear had gotten into all of it," said Longobardi. "It was uh-oh, so I started yelling at the cabin to make sure he wasn't still in there, because it was all fresh." So fresh that the grizzly had left flour-outlined paw prints in and around the cabin. The tracks left no doubt the bear was a grizzly.

Longobardi and Gilbert cautiously stepped up to the cabin and stood slack-jawed in the doorframe. Inside, the bear had been having the time of his life. He'd opened cabinet doors and emptied them of everything. When a cabinet door hadn't coop-erated, he'd just torn the entire cabinet off the wall. He'd pulled out the mattresses and yanked all the stuffing out of them.

Feathers from down sleeping bags were floating about. Pillows had been shaken to pieces. A fifty-five gallon drum that had been used to store grain for horses had been emptied. Canned meat and fish, pork and beans, peas, corn . . . every can in the place had been bitten open. "There was years of that old food, stuff that people should have packed out, beans and stuff that froze and thawed a thousand times," said Longobardi.

As Longobardi investigated, he noticed the padlock on the door was just placed in the hasp, unlocked, not locked down on the deadbolt where it should have been. In a flash, Longobardi understood what had happened. All the bear had had to do was give the door a little push and in he went. What the big grizzly found before his broad, sensitive nose was a bear banquet.

That incredible bear brain had learned a lesson and learned it the first time out. Push on something like a door and you'll get a treat. For the bear, thirteen years of so-called clean living came to a close with one simple, human screw-up.

For Longobardi and Gilbert, the worst was yet to come. They cleaned up the mess as best they could and then decided to go to the creek to fish out a cold one. "We said, well, let's go get our beer," said Longobardi. Unfortunately, the bear had been ahead of them. That incredible nose had found their beer beneath two feet of cold mountain stream. The bear had pulled out the feed sack, bitten into the entire twelve-pack one can at a time, and lapped up the suds.

"We were all ready," said Longobardi. "We'd been working for like seven days straight. We were just dreaming of these cold beers. So we were all bummed. I mean how he found those beers . . . ."

They didn't want to have anything to do with the Venus Creek cabin so they spent the night at a nearby outfitters camp. There they started to spread the word: grizzlies were in the territory. Everyone was going to have to learn how to bear camp.

Ironically, at about this same time, another grizzly in the Meeteetse country was raising hell with nearby cattle and sheep.

When Longobardi got home, he called up bear management specialist Mark Bruscino and told him there was grizz in the Greybull. "No one believed at that time that the odds of there being a grizzly bear there were very good at all," said Bruscino. But he found some bear hairs on the buck fence by the cabin and the hairs confirmed Longobardi's reading of the tracks.

"So we set a snare and we thought we'd at least catch it and get a radio collar on it since it was that far southeast, as far southeast as we had any grizzlies. One night I think he came back to the cabin. We actually stayed in the cabin like idiots and we heard something snorting outside, sniffing, outside the window, and we yelled, 'Get out of here!' The next morning there were bear tracks down by the spring, right below where the water comes in for the cabin."

Bruscino set up snares around the cabin but caught nothing. They spent four or five very enjoyable days in the September mountains, but the bear never returned after that first night.

Instead, the bear was a few drainages over, trashing an unoccupied outfitter's camp. There he got more food and learned more lessons that he wouldn't forget. For the next few years, the bear became something of a specialist. His counterpart in the Meeteetse country, Little Wahb, was a livestock-killing expert. This guy, however, focused on cabins. The parallels between the two bears were uncanny. Both were big males pioneering historic grizzly bear territory that had been vacant for sixty or more years. Both were destructive of human property. Both ranged back and forth across Carter Mountain, exploring both the Meeteetse side and the South Fork side of the Shoshone River. And both were seldom seen and very hard to capture.

"He was a very wary bear, nobody saw him that we are aware of," said Bruscino.

The cabin buster's *modus operandi* was always the same, push on something until it breaks and then get a food reward. Plus, the bear had a particularly destructive edge. He knocked over refrigerators and then jumped up and down on them until the doors sprung. He tore cupboards off the walls, chewed mattresses apart, and pulled debris far back into the woods. In several locations, he'd leave a steaming pile of bear crap in the midst of it all, almost as if he were making an editorial comment about cabins in bear country.

The grizzly sauntered to the top of Carter Mountain where he tore apart a sheep wagon, scattering its contents far and wide. He then trashed a cabin owned by the same rancher who was losing sheep to Little Wahb.

"This bear, unlike some, he knew just to take things apart. He was really kind of a demolition bear," said Bruscino. "A lot of bears will break a window out of a cabin, climb in and eat food, but they won't start taking things apart."

Then the cabin buster wandered into upper Meeteetse Creek where a couple of summer cabins had been built in "beautiful bear habitat," said Longobardi. One of these cabins was a flimsy affair in that state of perpetual construction that sometimes plagues summer cabins all over the mountains. Add some insulation one year, put in plumbing the next, add more stuff here and there, and never really get the job finished. This one was built mostly of particleboard and plywood. It had a roof and walls, but it wasn't really a mountain cabin that would have lasted years of big snows and tough winds. The big cabin-busting grizzly put it out of its misery.

Longobardi remembered getting that complaint. It came from the cabin's out-of-state owner, who reported the destruction of his dream mountain getaway. He said that bears were ripping the hell out of things. "I said, 'Well Geez Louise, a god-dang red squirrel could have torn that cabin apart.'"

When Longobardi and Bruscino went to investigate, they found out the owner hadn't been exaggerating. The bear had done the cabin in.

Inside the cabin, stairs led to a half loft. The bear climbed the stairs to the loft and then eased its way onto the open joists over the first story. Bruscino and Longobardi could read the story: the bear had slipped and fallen through the joists but caught himself and held onto a joist like he was doing chin-ups. For a while, the bear hung suspended in mid-air, digging its claws into the wood and clamping down on the joist with his mouth. Finally the mouthful broke loose and the bear fell to the first floor with a big chunk of two-by-eight in his jaws.

The bear climbed back up the stairs and still searched the place for food. "I think he learned that if you push on a door hard enough, it breaks and you get food and maybe if you push on a wall hard enough maybe it will break and you get food," said Bruscino. That's exactly what the bear did. It pushed on one of the outside walls from the inside and it pushed hard enough that the entire wall came loose and fell outside to the ground. "As near as we could tell, he did too."

They could see where the bear had landed atop the collapsed wall, and they could see some blood where the bear had cut its paw on a nail or something. Paw prints told the story.

"He ate everything in that cabin, just totally destroyed it," said Bruscino.

After that incident, the cabin buster went to the South Fork country and its collection of cabins, many of which are cowboy line-camps. On that side of the mountain, warden Tim Fagan was responsible for investigating bear-busted cabins. "He just never did it when there was someone around," said Fagan. "He just had reasoning ability. I mean that cabin-trashing bear, he could open doors, he could open oven doors. Once he'd break in, he'd open cabinets, but never do anything when people were around. He wasn't a threatening kind of bear. You know, it almost gives them personality."

There is no doubt that grizzlies have reasoning ability. Washington State's Dr. Robbins likes to tell this story: "There is a storage area above my bear pens where an eighty-year-old retired faculty member puttered around. There are small viewing windows in the floor that allow one to see what the bears are doing. One night he had been up there and he felt there was another presence in the room. He looked over and saw a bear's head as if it were mounted on the floor. A 500-pound male had heard him puttering around up there, gone outside and got a fifty-gallon drum and rolled it into the inside den. Then the bear stood the drum just underneath the viewing window, climbed up on it, popped off the viewing window, and stuck his head through so he could see what the old fart was doing. The bear couldn't climb all the way up, but he was just silently watching the professor."

Fagan and Bruscino did their best to trap the big male. They hauled a culvert trap to cabins that the bear trashed, but since they were remote, unoccupied mountain cabins, the owners sometimes didn't discover the damage until well after it had been done. Sometimes the bear wouldn't come back to the scene.

But sometimes he did. In the summer of 1994, the bear got into a line-camp cabin on the famed TE Ranch, managed by Curt Bales. "I had a neighbor that told me that something had broken into our cabin and we grabbed some plywood and stuff that had been around here and we took up there," said Bales.

Outside the door of the cabin was an uncapped and empty whiskey bottle. It had been full and capped inside a cabinet in the cabin. Apparently the bear had screwed off the cap and helped himself.

Bales boarded up all the windows and the door, but the bear returned later and got back into the cabin. Inside, he was even more destructive than the first time.

"Inside the cabin there was claw marks in the ceiling," said Bales. "It looked like the second time he broke into it, the door must have swung shut behind him because I mean he just trashed the cabin, and there was claw marks on the ceiling and stuff where he was trying to figure out how to get out of there."

Eventually he did get out and he made his way upstream to another cabin that had been built by Buffalo Bill Cody near the turn of the century. In late July, he was finally live-trapped there in a culvert trap. Bruscino used a jab stick to needle the big boar with tranquilizer. After the drug took effect, Bruscino snipped blue tags into each of the grizzly's ears and placed a radio collar around its neck. The fifteen-year old big boar weighed in at 470 pounds and now had an identity: number 226.

Bruscino was sure they had their culprit, the path of destruction was just so distinctive, but with a radio collar they could now be positive. They could give 226 another chance by moving him deep into the wilderness.

Bruscino hauled 226 into Yellowstone National Park, onto Blacktail Deer Plateau, miles away from the South Fork country and as far away from mountain cabins as was possible. By the time the bear was transported into the park, it had regained consciousness and was ready to get out. When Bruscino pulled the door open, 226 bolted into the forest. Bruscino hoped he wouldn't hear from the big male again and that he'd moved the bear well away from trouble.

Unfortunately, it wasn't far enough for 226. The truth is that what little wild country is left in the Lower Forty-Eight is sometimes not big enough for a grizzly, and for a bear that has learned a human-induced lesson, it's tough to get by peacefully. By fall, 226 had wandered east, out of the park, into Sunlight Basin where there are plenty of mountain cabins and even a ranch or two.

On the 7D Guest Ranch, 226 got into the ranch's main guest lodge in the middle of the night, waking one of the ranch's owners, David Dominick, out of a sound sleep in a nearby building. "I heard this crashing and I woke up," said Dominick. "My dog was asleep on the bed with me and she never moved. I thought, Oh, my God, we've got a bear."

Between the two-story cabin where Dominick was staying and the lodge was a small stream with a wooden bridge. The lodge itself has several wings, including a dishwashing area, dining room and laundry.

"I poked the flashlight out the window and sure enough, caught this bear in the flashlight," said Dominick. "I caught the bear just as it was entering the walkway from the dining room to the dishwashing area to the kitchen. I had the bear in the light and I screamed at the bear and evidently that was enough and the bear backed out and then took off."

Dominick was convinced the bear would come back so he found his Winchester pump 20-gauge shotgun and loaded it with birdshot. He took the screen off his bedroom window, set the loaded gun by the window, and went back to sleep.

The sound of breaking glass woke him a little bit later. He sat up and went to the window and saw the form of the bear moving along the side of the lodge. Aiming high, he let loose a round to scare the bear. The bear spun and ran across the bridge in the direction of the cabin and Dominick triggered another round. The grizzly spun again and ran around the corner of the lodge, and Dominick gave him a farewell salute with the 20-gauge.

It was the trademark entry of 226. He had ripped down a screen door, busted down the wooden door, and walked right in. Once inside, the bruin did extensive damage. Several large picture windows had been broken.

"He'd smashed windows out of the dishwashing area," said Dominick. "He'd gone all the way around to the laundry which was another door going into the main lodge, and he had ripped that door off and so there was all this damage all over the place. When I got in there I could see that the bear, instead of going through anything that he had ripped apart, he had smashed just a smallish side window next to the walkway door. He crawled through there. He'd cut his feet, so there was this big bloody paw mark going down the wall where he'd slipped in through. He'd gotten as far as a coffee can and he'd bitten through this coffee can and his saliva and his tooth marks was all over it. He had not gotten around the corner into the kitchen. Had he made that corner before I caught him with the flashlight, he would have been in the kitchen where the sugar was, where the flour was, the whole ball of wax."

Dominick had done some damage with his shotgun as well. "One of my rounds had gone right through and splattered all over the new Hobart dishwasher, and of course that news spread all over the Sunlight Basin and everybody thought that was just terrific that we had killed the dishwasher."

The next afternoon, warden Mac Black hauled a trap to the ranch and that night he caught a bear. Unfortunately, it wasn't the bear he was after. Instead, two grizzly cubs of the year were inside the trap and they weren't happy.

"The next morning I wake up early to this gawd-awful caterwauling and screaming and crying carrying on out there," said Dominick. "I call up Mac Black and I say, 'Mac, I think we've got a problem, you've got something trapped out there and they are really carrying on, there's an awful lot of crying and stuff going on.'"

Black called Bruscino, and when they pulled up to the trap, the cubs' mother charged the truck. Bruscino knew the mother and her cubs were "non-target" because Dominick had only seen one bear, and besides, he had a good fix on 226 with the radio receiver. The big male was definitely in the area.

Now Bruscino had a dilemma on his hands. He had cubs inside a trap, an aggressive and dangerous mother outside the trap, and no way to get to the trap to release the cubs.

"She wouldn't let us near the trap," said Bruscino. "When we tried to do something, she'd charge the truck and chase us back down the road." As time went by, Bruscino became worried about the health of the young cubs. He weighed his options. He could shoot the untrapped mother with a tranquilizer dart, a technique called "free-darting." Usually bear managers try to dart bears when they are caught in a snare so the bear can't run off before the drugs take effect. Free-darting definitely has its cons.

"Once they get hit by a dart, they take off. Then you lose them," said Bruscino. "I didn't want to free-dart her because there's a lot of heavy timber there. I'm not about to crawl in the trees with a half drugged grizzly bear."

Bruscino hauled another culvert trap to the site and set it up as close to the trapped cubs as the sow would let him. That didn't work either. "She'd just lie down at the base of that trap holding her cubs," said Bruscino, who watched from the safety of his truck. The family instinct in bears is a tight one, and while Bruscino was trying to figure out the next move, he saw evidence of just how tight. "She'd try to nurse the cubs. She'd stand up and try to put her nipples through the grate of the trap. It was cool." She'd also lie across the top of the trap, dangling all four legs off its sides.

Bruscino devised a new plan. It took a fair amount of manpower and equipment. Dominick, Black, and Gary Brown, another Wyoming Game and Fish Department employee, all played a role.

In their trucks the men approached the trap, and the bear came towards them. "As she approached she took a look at us," said Bruscino. "Gary was in position and I called him on the radio and I said, 'Just take a run at her and hit your siren and see if she'll move.'"

They did and she did. The sow ran down an old logging road with Brown chasing her in his truck. Dominick was in the passenger seat. Brown honked the horn, blasted the siren, flashed the lights, and bounced down the road with the sow ahead of the truck. At the same time and working quickly, Bruscino and Black drove to the trapped cubs, and while hanging out the window, Bruscino tied a rope onto the trap door. Then Black backed off while Bruscino held the rope, lifting the sliding door. The cubs bolted from the trap.

"Gary and I are driving down this road, bouncing this pickup all over the place, siren going, and the sow is going like hell," said Dominick. "Then these two cubs come streaking by us and join up with her and away they go."

"Sure enough, they reunited and all took off," said Bruscino. "She never came back." Neither did 226. Instead, he went over to yet another set of cabins in the Sunlight Basin.

In early November, 226 broke into a cabin on Dead Indian Pass. From this wind-swept pass, you can see the staggeringly beautiful crags of the North Absaroka Mountains and, to the far horizon, the Beartooth Plateau in Montana. The Sunlight Basin hugs the foreground, and the awesome dark chasm of the Clark Fork of the Yellowstone River cleaves the whole scene in half. This country is a mix of private and public lands; some pioneers were hardy enough to get all the way up past the canyon and stake out homesteads. Now many of these early homesteads have been cut up into cabin sites, dude ranches, and recreational camps. Northwestern Wyoming Community College has a summer field camp here. This is where 226 did some of his last and best work.

At the unoccupied Dead Indian cabin, Bruscino set a trap. Now there was snow on the ground, so Bruscino could read the story in the fresh powder. Several nights in a row, 226 came back and walked right around the trap.

"He walked around that trap several times and then got back into the cabin and did a lot of destruction," said Bruscino. "This is like a log home, this isn't a small little chintzy-built cabin, this thing is really built. He busted the door off and it was a good, stout, heavy outside door." That door was replaced by a very heavy, industrial steel shop door. It didn't last the night. The grizzly pushed on it so hard that it buckled and popped out of the doorframe.

Then the bear made its way over to the college field camp, got into some unoccupied cabins there, and went up into more cabins behind the camp. "There were hunters in some of those cabins," said Bruscino. "He would walk up to those buildings where there were hunters, and he wouldn't attempt to get in them. It's extremely rare for a bear to try and break into an occupied cabin, almost unheard of is how rare it is."

But the bear did get into another unoccupied cabin several nights in a row. There, he was up to his usual tricks, trashing things and eating what he could. It was nearing the time when 226 would go into hibernation, and like all bears at that time of year, the big grizzly was in a feeding frenzy.

"He was packing stuff up into the trees, including some dried spaghetti, a bag of beans, and a few jars of other stuff," said Bruscino. "There was also a bunch of those big gallon wide-mouth jars full of candy. He packed three of those up into this little spruce patch and he literally sat there and fiddled with those jars of candy and unscrewed the lids and ate the contents, where he could have easily just busted them. They were just glass jars."

Bruscino was now absolutely positive it was 226. He had a good radio fix on the bear and the methods were the same: patience for things like unscrewing jar lids and whiskey bottle caps, busted doors, and complete destruction elsewhere.

Bruscino set up a snare in some low-growing, wind-battered krummholz and baited the snare with part of a lamb. "I went to town and I got a three pound bag of M&Ms, and in the snow, I put a line of M&Ms from the front door of that cabin to the snare."

That night, the bear came again to the cabin. The tracks in the snow were like reading a book. "He hit that line of M&Ms and his tracks followed them," said Bruscino. "He picked up every one of them, licked them up out of the snow. There were just these little red and yellow and green dots and melted M&M shell and his footprints."

In the snare was 226, and this time, his career as a cabin buster was over. Bruscino had the distasteful job of putting him down with a dose of euthanol. The bear was fifteen years old and he had put on nearly 100 pounds since his capture in July, tipping the scales at 544 pounds.

"He lived successfully in the wild until he got into that Venus Basin cabin and got a hell of a food reward," said Bruscino. "Then he had it figured out. That's how important it is not let these bears get fed."

After 226 broke into the Venus Creek cabin, it was completely bear-proofed. Nowadays, almost every hunting camp in the Greybull River country has cleaned up its act and is bear camping. The Wyoming Game and Fish Department has a cabin over the hill from the Venus Basin cabin on Jack Creek. Longobardi personally bear-proofed that cabin, complete with steel shutters and a steel outside door.

"Jack Creek is a good set up," said Bruscino. "That's the way to protect your property. Certainly you never want to store any attractants outside, things like garbage. Leave that stuff inside and pack it out with you when you leave at the end of your stay. It's real important not to leave anything smelly in there, food or garbage. Then a good set of steel shutters that have tight seams is a real plus in bear country. They can't get their claws in there and pull the shutter open and break a window out."

Anything less can wind up with some serious property damage—and a dead bear. 226 paid with his life and property owners all over the range paid for the damage, all because of one slip-up.

"It was a total space job that ended with this bear getting killed," said Longobardi.

One-o-four, the crowd pleaser

Bears and busy highways don't mix, even for an incredibly tolerant mother grizzly

Jim Hamilton knew she was a special bear the first time he saw her. He could tell by the way that she looked. Other bears looked other ways. Some just didn't look like the kind of bear that you'd want to be standing on the same ground at the same time with. He'd been bluff charged a few times by those kinds of bears, and even when he was sitting in his big, faded-red van with a spring-melt river between him and that kind of bear, a charge like that took his breath away. But this bear was different. This bear was special.

Everyone knew her. How couldn't they? She was bear number 104. Say it real fast and it sounds like a name, One-o-four. Some people called her Brown Eyes, a name almost implying sweetness, gentleness, qualities definitely unfitting for a mother grizzly bear with cubs, unless you happened to be one of those cubs. Other people called her Arnie, nicknamed after Arnold Palmer, the famous golfer with the smiling eyes, the crowd pleaser. Hamilton just called her One-o-four.

She was quite probably the most photographed wild grizzly bear in the world. She was the most productive known female bear in the entire Yellowstone region. And she lived her whole life along a major U.S. highway. The music that accompanies the lives of many grizzlies is that of the wild: booming rivers, bugling elk, drumming grouse, singing wind. One-o-four's life was accompanied almost daily by the humming of automobile and truck tires up and down U.S. Highway 14-16-20, the North Fork Highway to the east entrance of Yellowstone National Park. The tourists coming to Yellowstone every year—a number around three million in 2002—might spend an entire vacation in the park without seeing what they really wanted to see, a grizzly bear. But when they pointed their cars toward the east and passed out of the park, One-o-four made many a trip unforgettable.

The vision of your first wild grizzly burns so deeply into your memory cells that it is unwashable, indelible, untouchable. You can focus it, change the depth of field, enhance its quality, but you cannot brush it away. It is on the film of your life. Old men nearing death will see that grizzly bear in their mind-film before they will see images of their own grandchildren, even if that film is old and faded by sixty, seventy years of exposure to other memories.

One-o-four is burned into a lot of human brains. One of them is Jim Hamilton's. Frequent travelers on the North Fork Highway know his red van. It will be pulled over on the wide shoulder of the highway, and when they see it, they invariably slow down in that most Yellowstone of manners. If you've traveled the Yellowstone country you'll know that a car pulled to the side of the road means slow down and start looking into the woods for wildlife. Nowhere else on the planet does a car on a shoulder of a highway cause so much reaction. If you see the red van, you'll know that there's a good chance that a wild animal is nearby and the man inside the van is burning up film in his camera. For many years when the red van was parked on the North Fork Highway, it meant that One-o-four was around.

"I really liked that bear," said Hamilton. "She was awesome. Just her nature and her behavior with her cubs, she'd play with them for hours sometimes."

For twenty years or more, Hamilton has prowled the Yellowstone country and particularly the North Fork Highway, shooting photographs. A printer by trade, he'd leave for the North Fork after work and eat a cold dinner in his van, driving up the road, looking for wildlife. Weekends would find him doing more of the same, driving, spotting wild animals, stopping, shooting pictures. It became his life's passion. The printing press paid the bills, but the pictures gave him purpose. One of the pictures he is most proud of was published in the National Geographic book, *Yellowstone Country, The Enduring Wonder*. The picture is One-o-four, the sunlight sparkling off her blonde hide, flanked by two cubs standing on their hind legs. All three bears are peering intently at something only they can see.

The North Fork Highway runs like a huge, life-giving artery between Cody and the east entrance to Yellowstone National Park. Teddy Roosevelt once called it one of the most scenic highways in America. In many ways, the highway is indeed an artery, a byway for tourism dollars that pump into the economy of Cody and Park County. In the peak season, as many as 5,000 vehicles travel this road in a single month. But for most bears, the highway is exactly the opposite of life giving.

Roads and wildlife don't mix. Roads and grizzly bears in particular don't mix. The North Fork Highway pulses through a corridor that bear biologists call a population sink. Grizzlies that walk into this area often sink right out of sight. A lot of bears die along highways and the North Fork is one of the deadliest. It's not the highway so much as it what it brings. Bears do end up as road-kill, but more often bears get into other kinds of trouble. Highways mean people and in the case of the North Fork, quite a few people. There are a half dozen major tourist lodges up and down the highway lining the banks of the North Fork of the Shoshone River and its tributaries. There are double that number of campgrounds, and no small number of summer cabins. There's a Boy Scout Camp. And this is all within the boundaries of the Shoshone National Forest. On private land there's even more development.

Fair or unfair, the truth is that the North Fork is a place where bears, both black and grizzly, don't last very long. Except one very special grizzly bear. She lived two decades along the busy highway and she was good at it.

One-o-four's base of operations was Pahaska Tepee, the famous lodge that had been built by the legendary Buffalo Bill Cody in 1901. Former Wyoming bear biologist Larry Roop caught her in a culvert trap behind Pahaska Tepee on Crow Creek in 1984. At the time, she was just two and a half years old. Biologists like Roop were very interested in roadside bears and wanted to keep a handle on their movements for a number of reasons, not the least of which was human safety. By radio collaring and ear-tagging her, Roop hoped to get some idea of where she was going and when. He punched green tags into each ear, placed a radio collar around her neck, and let her go.

"I'd say the phenomenon of roadside bears started in the late 1970s and then through the 1980s because we started getting more bears," said Roop. By the time One-o-four entered the Yellowstone bear scene, it looked to many biologists as if grizzly bears were making a comeback. Roop explained: "The more dominant bears start using the habitat back away from the roadside, and the less dominant bears discover that they are not bothered a lot by other bears if they feed along the roadsides. In fact, their niche is not only roadsides but it's daytime. All of which is not typical for a grizzly bear's behavior. But this helps them avoid conflict with more dominant bears."

By the time One-o-four was first captured, she had become something of a fixture in the Pahaska area, and she and an untagged female that Roop thought was her sibling were seen many times that summer and the next. Sometimes she was blamed for causing trouble, and she was likely getting some human foods.

But One-o-four was not acting aggressively like some other bears. In 1986 she was stopping traffic all summer and fall with twin cubs of the year. There were reports of people approaching her to within fifteen feet. That's not a typo. *Fifteen feet.* Many grizzly mothers will bluff charge humans if they get within 100 yards. Some really protective ones will bluff charge people who get within 300 yards. That's 900 feet. One-o-four was letting camera-packing tourists get within fifteen feet. And she was ignoring them while munching on roadside clover.

Bear managers knew that they were sitting on a ticking time bomb. "We often worried that someone was going to get injured," said Roop. In October of that year, another sow grizzly, 59, killed and ate the better part of a 38-year-old Great Falls, Montana, auto mechanic named Bill Tesinsky. An avid hunter who fancied himself a photographer, Tesinsky had approached 59 in Yellowstone National Park. Park rangers found the half of him that the bear didn't eat, and they shot 59 as she was feeding on the remains. Rangers also found Tesinky's camera and tried to reconstruct the episode from the film and the physical scene. As near as they could tell, Tesinsky had essentially stalked this bear—who didn't have cubs—to within thirty to fifty feet before she had enough.

The fact that One-o-four was letting black-sock-wearing, Bermuda-short-clad yo-yos get within fifteen feet was absolutely staggering. Grizzlies can run twice as fast as humans, and at fifteen feet, they can be on you faster than you can read these words.

It wasn't only the out-of-state tourists. A Cody photographer caused a lot of trouble. He was one of those so-called bulletproof types who think they are invincible. He was getting way too close to One-o-four. On foot.

"I'll bet this guy shot up fifty or sixty rolls of film on One-o-four and he just hounded her," said Roop. "We had problems with him all the time and we'd tell him to stay back and leave her alone and he wouldn't."

In one case, One-o-four and her cubs were feeding on a road-killed deer in some willows just off the highway. Anyone with any mountain sense will tell you that the two most dangerous situations with any bear, black or grizzly, are a mother with cubs and a bear on a carcass. Here was One-o-four with both.

"This guy would approach within fifty or sixty feet, taking pictures," said Roop. "He was just as belligerent as heck. He didn't like anybody telling him what to do. He was just getting terribly close, and as docile and non-aggressive as she was, she had cubs there and they are feeding on a carcass. I mean no other bear in the world would have tolerated that."

Most photographers knew to stay in their vehicles and not push the bears. But even in vehicles, many bear experts believe photographers habituate bears to humans. Creep your vehicle close to a bear to take a photograph and eventually the bear learns that vehicles aren't a threat. They become, in a sense, habituated.

One-o-four was also habituating humans to bears. If a man can approach one bear so close, why can't he approach all bears that close? This is not something new; Yellowstone National Park had been seeing human habituation to bears during its entire history. The great naturalist Olaus J. Murie warned officials of it in a paper published in 1944. It's called complacency.

One-o-four started hanging out at campgrounds and lodges. Living may be a little easier for a while at such places, but the high life wears thin eventually. These aren't good places for bears, they are bad places. Hamilton once shot several pictures of One-o-four while she was doing the breaststroke right through the middle of an open sewage treatment pond.

"That really degraded her," said Hamilton. "Of course you know they eat anything, they do anything, and there was an aerosol can of paint floating and she grabbed that and brought it to the bank and bit it. It blew up in her face and she got paint on her and she went over backwards and run off. Then she came back. She chewed the can into little bits and licked up the paint. There was blood on the can even, where she cut herself."

It was little things like this that had the people in charge of bear management very concerned. While the sewage pond was later enclosed with a bear-proof, electric fence, One-o-four was still hanging around and getting an occasional food reward. She wasn't really damaging anything or hurting anyone, but it was probably just a matter of time. The wildlife folks knew they had to do something.

At the time, bear managers were experimenting with a number of techniques to keep bears away from humans. One of these was an aversive conditioning study that was initiated at Pahaska and other lodges by several researchers in the mid-1980s. One of these researchers was Carrie Hunt, who would go on to some notoriety for using Karelian bear dogs to chase away problem bears. Another researcher was Wyoming Game and Fish Department warden Kirk Inberg, who, along with another biologist and a pilot, would lose his life in an airplane crash while tracking a radio collared bear in the Wyoming wilderness in 1991.

The study by Inberg and Hunt called for long hours and work around the clock. Using night vision goggles and guns with infrared sights, the idea was to shoot problem bears with what amounted to a water-filled, plastic bullet that didn't penetrate the skin. The impact would whack the bear hard enough to make it stay out of the area. Just like Pavlov tinkled a bell to get his dogs to come to dinner, this study tried something quite the opposite. If a bear was seen approaching the dumpsters at Pahaska, researchers would start playing birdcalls, quail or woodpecker calls, through loudspeakers mounted on their truck. If the bear still came in, the shooter, sometimes placed in a tree stand elsewhere, would use a gun called a "Bear Thumper" and hammer the bear with one of these bullets. If a bear's life was made miserable around a human place, it might save the bear from becoming habituated or change its behavior after it had gotten some human food reward.

After several years of study, it was determined that in many cases this kind of aversive condition was not particularly effective. But there was at least one bear that was positively impacted, so to speak. It was One-o-four. In late 1986 and early 1987, One-o-four was hammered a couple of times with the Thumper gun.

"Bears that were more dominant like aggressive males or more adult bears—we got mixed results on," said Roop. "But with a bear like her, it immediately altered her behavior. She quit coming around the camp areas and around the campgrounds. I think it was a bad experience for her and she learned quickly to avoid bad experiences. She had had some food habituation, but not enough, so we ended up that she was a good bear."

In 1987, One-o-four was captured twice and moved deep inside Yellowstone National Park, but she always came back home. These moves may have been part of the reason that she never caused trouble in the North Fork area again.

During her life, One-o-four was captured and released six times. All but two of these were for research purposes. But she was very wise to traps and only entered a culvert trap twice in her life: in 1984 the first time she was caught and in 1992 the last time she was caught. For bear researchers to keep a radio collar on her—radio collars often slip off of bears—they had to resort to different methods of capture. One of these was the free-dart technique, and because One-o-four was so easy to approach in a vehicle, she got shot twice while she was grazing roadside.

"She went for a while without a collar and we were trying to get a collar back on her," said Roop. "I was going into the park for a meeting on Sylvan Pass and all I had was a drug pistol. Well those are normally what you would use for a bear in a trap; they are fairly short range, just a little CO_2 powered pistol. But I get up to Sylvan Pass and there's One-o-four, right there in that meadow just before Sylvan Lake. So I get my dart loaded up and I lobbed that dart over a log, shot her from about forty yards. It dropped over that log and hit her in the rump and she wandered out into that meadow and keeled over."

Roop was able to get a collar back on her and record some data while One-o-four's twin cubs sat on their haunches and watched. Then he backed off and waited until she came around and wandered off with her cubs.

Eventually, after this kind of treatment from humans, One-o-four got wise.

"In most of the later years One-o-four was really a little bit more stand-offish than she was when she was younger," said Roop, who even after he retired from the Wyoming Game and Fish Department would still drive up the North Fork to look for her. "She would kind of hang back. You would see her and her yearlings or her cubs but she was not really like some of her offspring, she would not let people get that close. She would move off and she would stay in the same general area and people would see her and report her all the time. But with One-o-four, if people stopped on the road and showed up, she would start moving off and go into the timber. She was around, but not that approachable."

This was particularly true when wildlife biologists came around, because One-o-four would see the dark green Wyoming Game and Fish Department vehicles and move off into the distance. She had been habituated to recognize and avoid these vehicles.

"I absolutely believe that she recognized me. A lot of managers have had that experience where the bears just recognize you and your vehicle," said Bruscino, who noted that one bear manager doing aversive conditioning in British Columbia would have to hide in the backseat of his daughter's car in order to shoot one particularly wise bear.

Some photographers had no problem maneuvering within range for a good photograph, particularly Hamilton. For two decades, Hamilton wandered up and down the North Fork Highway, often shooting picture after picture of One-o-four. He knew her habits and he knew where he was likely to find her from day to day. Among his collection are incredible shots of One-o-four lying on her back nursing her cubs, One-o-four feeding on a carcass, One-o-four playing with her cubs. All of these shots were taken from his vehicle.

One-o-four drew crowds even if she was a little distant from the road. Sometimes fifty or more vehicles stopped along the highway. Most people stayed in their vehicles, but Hamilton witnessed some people getting too close. He tried to police them a bit, but it was hard to change human behavior, perhaps harder than it is to change bear behavior. At one point, Hamilton watched a well-known videographer essentially chase her all day long. "He went clear down into Sylvan Meadows following her one day," said Hamilton. "She couldn't stop and nurse her cubs or anything. He was a self-appointed bear person."

Through her life, One-o-four had eight cubs. After being weaned, most of the cubs would go on foraging along the highway. Other than one aggressive female and possibly a big aggressive male known as Commando, her cubs were all docile, roadside bears, but none were as successful with roadside living as their mother was. Time and again, she proved just how tolerant she was of people. And of dogs.

Bob Coe has lived on the North Fork all his life. His father bought the lodge at Pahaska Tepee in 1946, and today, Bob runs it. One day, One-o-four was walking in front of the old lodge at Pahaska Tepee. She had a cub and was casually moving along, grazing on grass, minding her own business, when Coe's dog attacked.

"My dog jumped out of the truck and went over and tried to chase her and got in between her and her cub," said Coe. "She took off after that dog and swiped him and he ran clear across the property and jumped in the back of the truck and laid down. She took the cub and went the other way. It was just a little warning swipe. She was a great bear, we never had any problems with her, not a one."

One time Bruscino and his wife and dog were hiking in the North Fork when they rounded a bend in the trail and walked right up on One-o-four and her cubs. The bear just casually sauntered off.

Once a sow that was likely One-o-four got into a fight with a boar right in the middle of the highway in front of Pahaska Lodge. "The boar was down in the meadow and One-o-four had taken her cub up out of the meadow and was going above the highway," said Coe. People were everywhere, watching these bears, not knowing just how dangerous the situation really was. Biologists aren't sure why, but male grizzlies are one of the chief predators of young cubs, and sows have died trying to defend them.

"He bolted up the hill and right through the people and they had a tussle in the middle of the highway and spun around fighting," said Coe. The bears ran right through the middle of the crowd. "People were running everywhere. Pretty soon the boar had enough and he went down below the hill and she went up the hill and brought her cub back down into the meadow later and they went on. But the people running, that was really something."

There are dozens of stories like this of One-o-four. She definitely made her mark on the North Fork people, tourists and locals alike. "I think she's one of those legend bears because she was tied to humans and so many people knew about her and she was so observable," said Roop. "People followed her from year after year."

She was never a very big bear either, averaging less than 200 pounds each time she was trapped. But she endured. "One-o-four was just a favorite bear," said Coe. "A real favorite bear."

In the late 1990s, the North Fork Highway underwent a massive widening and straightening, a multi-million dollar construction project. Highway officials said the volume of traffic was too much for the old road and a new design was needed. It was incredibly controversial and several conservation groups and individuals fought the project every step of the way.

The speed limit on the new highway was kept low because of wildlife, including moose, bison, elk and bears, but it was now easier for drivers to go a little faster because the road was wider and straighter. Inevitably the project made the North Fork even more of a population sink for grizzly bears.

In May 2001, professional photographer Jim Yule saw One-o-four and her sole cub that year in the meadows near Pahaska Tepee. Yule, who hails from Worland, Wyoming, was just starting to shoot pictures on the North Fork, having spent several previous years inside the park. This was the first time and the last time he would get quality pictures of the famous bear. For a long time, he sat in his truck and shot film while One-o-four played with her cub.

"She tackled her cub to the ground and wrestled with him and then she found a garbage bag and she just laid on her back and played with it," said Yule. "Then the cub jumped on her and then she would attack her cub and they'd play fight and stuff like that. She'd just be a tolerant bear that would walk around the edges with her cubs and stuff and browse and she'd never even give you a look hardly. That's what made her such a good bear. She wasn't interested in people and yet she really didn't mind being around them."

Late the next night, a young man was driving his small pickup past Pahaska Tepee when he felt his truck hit something solid just as he was crossing the new, high bridge over Pahaska Creek, within a stone's throw of Buffalo Bill's old lodge. The radiator burst and the bumper buckled and his little pickup shuddered and died. The man stopped and looked behind him.

One-o-four lay dead in the middle of the road. The man hadn't even seen her.

In the dark the bear carcass was loaded into the back of Cody game warden Craig Sax's vehicle and taken to the department's office on the edge of town. The next morning, Bruscino and Gary Brown started to look it over, not realizing what bear it was. It had been a year or two since Bruscino had seen her. Bears that don't cause much trouble don't get much attention from bear managers, so Bruscino thought that One-o-four may have just disappeared and died. She was old now and past her most productive years. Some of her teeth were in bad shape.

"No one realized it had an ear tag until Gary and I looked and shit, it was One-o-four," said Bruscino.

Getting scraped off the new concrete of a highway bridge was an inglorious end for a pretty amazing bear. One-o-four's death made the front page of the *Casper Star-Tribune*, the state's largest newspaper, and headlines around the region. Folks at Pahaska held a wake of sorts for her. One-o-four had become the first grizzly bear fatality of the fancy new highway. She had died where she'd lived for nineteen successful years.

Were the story to end here, perhaps that would be enough. But the legend of One-o-four has near-mythic status. One-o-four died on May 14, 2001, in front of Buffalo Bill Cody's famous old lodge after being hit by a truck driven by a man named—and I'm not making this up—Billy Buffaloe.

Jim Hamilton doesn't remember who came to his house or what he was doing, but he does remember how he felt when he heard the news that One-o-four was dead. "There was kind of a hole in my heart," he said. "You know, I'd been around her so much."

Bruscino went to the accident site and heard that during the accident, One-o-four's yearling cub had jumped off the bridge and down onto the rocks beside Pahaska Creek, a drop of some twenty feet. The young bear reportedly was seen that morning but had limped off. Later that fall, the year-ling was seen again, limping. The next year, a bear matching his description came to Pahaska and hung around. Instantly, the lodge crew named him High Dive. It had to be the same bear, One-o-four's last cub. Even Bruscino felt that way. So did Jim Yule.

"I'm positive that was her cub," said Yule. "It was the right age and looked and acted just like her."

Yule spent about twenty days in 2002 watching the young bear. He called him Little Four, but most of the people at Pahaska called him High Dive. Like his mother, the young bear was incredibly tolerant of people, even more tolerant of people than his mother had been. And people were just as stupid as they had been with her. Maybe even stupider.

"I've seen people within three feet of him," said Yule, who now works with a movie camera and has recorded this kind of lunacy on film. "You know, kneeling down to take pictures with a little camera. Three feet, eight feet. That bear was kind of skin and bones, but his arms were still built."

And he was still dangerous. Photographers—professional, amateur, and tourist—are sometimes guided by questionable ethics. A good picture is a prize and a prize causes greed, whether that prize is just a snapshot in a photo album or a valuable cover shot for some glossy magazine. Some photographers will buy an inexpensive scanner at any electronics store and use that scanner to hone in on radio-collared bears. Any scanner that can pick up a radio frequency can pick up the steady pulse of a radio collar on a grizzly. With a directional antenna, you can even deduce not only that the bear is nearby, but roughly where. Then you wait for your photo.

For the most part, Yule has seen good ethics among the pros, but there are those few who will leave their vehicles and sneak around the roadside bears to try to get the good sun angle.

"You would just be astonished if you saw some of the things they do with these roadside bears," said Yule. "You know, you take what you got, you just hope the bear moves and you can move your vehicle to a different and safer location to shoot from. Most photographers will help police, but again there's that percentage. You'll have ten photographers out there and there's always that one guy who has to be an idiot."

The spring of 2003, it didn't take High Dive long to get into trouble. He was hanging out at Pahaska and was virtually immovable. He was hanging out on cabin porches and some people were afraid to come out of their cabins to go down to dine at the lodge. Coe called Bruscino.

Bruscino drove up the North Fork and found the bear back behind the lodge where the dude horses are kept. He was asleep right in the middle of the dirt road, but he woke up when a wrangler showed up with a horse she had just purchased at an auction. Immediately High Dive started to climb into the corral with the horse.

"I've never seen a bear act like that around a horse," said Bruscino. "He was in really poor condition, he'd just obviously come out of hibernation."

The wrangler made the obvious decision to not leave the horse there, and Bruscino worked up a plan. He'd shoot crackershells, which are essentially huge firecrackers that are fired out of a shotgun and explode near the target. He launched a few at the bear, but High Dive just jumped to one side and went back to what he was doing. Bruscino couldn't move him.

After investigating a little more, it was revealed the bear had taken nine full beers off a cabin porch that a lamebrain had left outside. Moreover, Yule claimed that one of the lodge employees was shooting ground squirrels and the bear was hanging around and eating them.

"He never—and everybody I'd talk to would say the same thing—he'd never be at the same place long," said Yule, who had watched him for nearly a month in 2002 and ten days in 2003 before the bear got into trouble at Pahaska. "He'd be at this pull out one day and then a mile down the river the next day and then he'd loop around and keep doing this continuous loop. Then you've some moron leaving beer out and leaving squirrels just seeing if the bear would come and eat them and then the bear all of a sudden just becomes totally dependent on that. Jesus H, that's terrible. It's crazy."

The lesson would be the same old saw: a fed bear is a dead bear. For Bruscino, it's an incredibly frustrating business because all it takes is one fool among one thousand. He hauled a culvert trap to the site and caught High Dive that very night.

The next morning Bruscino weighed the options. It was early spring, too early to get far enough into the high country to release the bear where it and humans would be safe. The weather was too poor for a helicopter to lift the young bear into the backcountry. He had a badly habituated bear that was letting people get within three feet. Young males are the least important bear to the overall health of the grizzly population. He'd seen bears like this make the same mistake time and again and be moved time and again. He called the Interagency Grizzly Bear Committee, the group tasked with overseeing the recovery of the Yellowstone grizzly bear population. They talked it over and the decision was made.

While the bear was still tranquilized, Bruscino pulled High Dive out of the trap and found his femoral artery. The bear was small, less than 190 pounds and in extremely poor condition with no body fat. Bruscino injected eighteen ccs of euthanol into the young bear's artery and waited. Quietly, High Dive took one last breath.

Irony had shadowed One-o-four and her cubs with the kind of oddity that makes goose bumps tingle your arms. High Dive drew his last breath of sweet mountain air within a few hundred feet of the place where, almost two years earlier to the exact day, his mother had died. Even stranger was the date: May 11, 2003...Mother's Day.

That High Dive lived only three years and his mother lived nineteen in the same country was a study in bear personalities. It was also, perhaps, a harbinger of things to come. For photographers like Yule, it meant possibly the last of the roadside bears.

Other than a dark male that Yule calls the Commando bear, he felt that by 2003 all of One-o-four's cubs were dead. Of course those bears had successfully raised cubs of their own and One-o-four's genes were likely still going, but One-o-four's cubs themselves were all probably gone.

Yule rattled them off: 318 shot by Wisconsin hunters, 380 euthanized, the runt bear hit by a car, and Little Four. The

Commando bear, though, was a big dominant, elusive male and it would not stay long along the highway. The highway meant death, even for little One-o-four.

"She taught them to use the roadway to their advantage for safety and it got them killed," said Yule. "She trusted humans for her own safety and that was her demise."

The continuing legacy of One-o-four

Today, the legacy of bear 104 lives on in the first American natural history museum established in the 21st century. You can find her in the popular Mountain Meadow Environment at the Draper Museum of Natural History, Cody, Wyoming, helping visitors understand the complex relationships between humans and nature in the Greater Yellowstone Area. Her last cub will soon join her in the immersive exhibition. Their lives have ended, but their presence will continue to inspire generations of Draper Museum visitors with the wonder of wild Wyoming.

Draper Museum of Natural History
Buffalo Bill Historical Center
720 Sheridan Ave.
Cody, WY 82414
Phone: 307-587-4771
www.bbhc.org

"It was a surgical strike."

An inside look at Yellowstone's most baffling bear attack

Imagine you are a park ranger in Yellowstone, the nation's first national park. It's a great job. The best job in the world. This is your ninth summer and the wild backcountry calls you. You know it well; you've even written a trail guide that can be purchased in the park's bookstores. Your experience is tapped for many things: searches, rescues, expertise. So you get this call. It's the last day of July 1984.

You talk to a man and his wife. They are very nice people. Very concerned. The man's sister failed to meet them at the Pelican Creek trailhead. Worry stitches across the man's face. In less than a month, his sister will be twenty-six. She was backpacking alone on just a short overnight foray and was scheduled to meet her brother and his wife this afternoon. She's now two and a half hours overdue. You quietly interview the brother, asking all the right questions, asking about his sister's experience, about her gear, about where she's permitted to camp, everything that you can think of and everything you've been trained to ask.

Park protocol calls for waiting twenty-four hours before activating a search and rescue. It's a policy that makes sense from an administrative point of view. A lot of people who "go missing" in the park usually just get confused or they lose track of time in the splendor of the park or the fishing, or their watch quits working, or any of a bunch of reasons, and eventually they show up where they were supposed to be, hours late.

Maybe this is the case too. You ask the couple to go back to the trailhead and you assure them the National Park Service will check from time to time. But something is already tingling in the back of your mind. For some reason, this doesn't sound like one of those cases. It gnaws at you. The area where this solo hiker went is open country and the trail is fairly straightforward. This woman is experienced and she's never late. She's close to your age and likes to hike alone in the woods. So do you.

You make radio contact with a ranger who is staying in the Pelican Springs patrol cabin, several miles from where this woman was permitted to camp. He spends the last hour of darkness looking for the woman but doesn't find her. During the night, rangers check the trailhead several times. The young woman doesn't show up.

You get up before dawn and in the cool mist of a mountain morning on the first day of a new month, you saddle a horse. Not just any horse, but probably the park's best horse, a gelding with a buckskin hide and the disposition of a yellow Lab. Baldy is the Thorofare ranger's horse and the Thorofare is back in there, way back in there. A backcountry ranger needs a really dependable horse, one that doesn't mind riding the trails alone, one that isn't going to shy at something in the woods and leave you twisted and damaged at the side of some remote trail. Baldy is steady. His keeper, the Thorofare ranger, is on leave for a few days, but his horse is still on duty.

By seven you are on the trail heading up Pelican Creek into Pelican Valley. It is still wet from a series of rains the night before and dew clings to the grass and the wildflowers, sparkling in the morning sunlight. Baldy splashes through puddles and stretches it out. The trail is clean and unmarked, like a school blackboard awaiting the first stroke of chalk.

It's quiet and calm with nothing but the sounds of Baldy's hooves thumping hollowly on the trail and the occasional peaceful snort from the good horse as he steps out and warms up his big muscles. You ride for a while in sunlight and shadow and then Baldy steps out into the full morning sun and the broad valley of Pelican Creek. The valley stretches before you and you ride focused, looking for boot tracks, sweeping your eyes across the meadow. But there are no tents in the open or at the edges of the timber.

You ride in silence in the wide expanse of Pelican Valley and then you see a hiker in the distance, approaching you on the same trail. Baldy sees him too, and he rides easily, his ears perked. The horse misses nothing. As you get closer, you see it's a man, not the woman you are looking for. You know him; he volunteers for park searches. He's also been out looking for the solitary hiker but he hasn't seen her. But he has seen a grizzly, a big one, probably 500 pounds, walking south from the Astringent Creek area into the Pelican Valley not fifteen minutes earlier.

Eventually Baldy carries you to the junction where the Astringent Creek trail heads north while the main trail runs east. You go north, riding into more timber as you follow Astringent Creek up toward Fern Lake.

Here you pick up tracks. They aren't human tracks. They are deep and perfect on the rain-washed trail and absolutely unmistakable. Grizzly, a big one. It's not unusual or alarming; after all, the Pelican Valley is some of the finest grizzly habitat in the whole park. Far to the east, in an old lookout tower atop Pelican Cone, a young man named Kerry Gunther is doing his master's project on grizzly bears, studying bear interaction with humans and bear predation on elk calves. With a telescope and a good view of a lot of country, Gunther has documented sixteen different bears using this country this summer. The tracks are headed out on the same trail you are riding in.

The young lady was issued a permit to camp at 5B1, a camp-site near Fern Lake, so you are surprised when you see a green tent at the edge of a meadow near White Lake. It's such an idyllic scene, a tent at the edge of a meadow and a branch of White Lake behind. From her brother's description, you know the tent belongs to the woman you are looking for. Maybe she got confused and ended up camping down here. Maybe she is hiking out this morning. The trail goes right past the campsite, 5W1, and so you ride Baldy over to say hello.

Twenty yards from the tent, Baldy skids to a stop, planting all four feet. He is scared. It totally catches you off guard. Baldy just plain doesn't act like this. He's seen hundreds of tents in his life and ridden miles and miles of these kinds of trails. He's grazed in the same meadows as elk and moose and even griz-zlies. Baldy is normally calm, solid, steady, balanced. But noth-ing you can do will make him go any closer. Finally you give up and dismount. He's rattled and blows air through his nostrils in that purring alarm that horses make when something both-ers them. He wants to get out of there and he spins in circles. You try not to get stepped on by the snorting, stamping horse while you tie him to a tree well away from the campsite. What is up with Baldy? The horse's behavior sets you on edge.

You walk toward the tent. It's a dome tent, set up perfectly at the campsite, only about thirty feet off the trail. Its door faces west and your shadow plays out before you as you walk to it, the sun warm on your back. When you step to the front of the tent, you notice the red-orange sleeping bag. It's laid out in front of the tent as if drying in the morning sun.

Then you notice the rip in the tent fly. It runs vertically. There's a rip in the tent door too. You bend down and look inside. Through the gaping hole, you see a neat pile of clothing and gear—a sleeping pad, a pen, a journal, a camera—all per-fectly undisturbed. It looks like the ideal backcountry scene, as if the owner had gotten up at dawn, stretched and yawned into the morning, pulled her sleeping bag into the sun to rid it of dew, and then taken a stroll into the beautiful meadow.

But there are rips in the tent and your heart drums. You start looking around. Just beyond the sleeping bag, you find something. It's a clump of human hair, blonde-brown, and then just beyond that is a bit of flesh. Only later is it identified as a piece of human lip.

Your heart leaps and every sense jumps into action. You draw your .357 magnum revolver from its holster. And you start calling the woman's name: "Brigitta? Brigitta? Hello? Brigitta?"

Ranger Mark Marschall remembers that day in 1984, that shining, perfect first day of August in the beautiful Yellowstone backcountry. He remembers those details. He wasn't imagining them. It was all very real. He had taken the report of the missing hiker, Brigitta Fredenhagen of Basel, Switzerland, from her brother, Andreas, the night before. Andreas was calm, soft-spoken, and spoke fluent English.

Now Marschall stood looking at what lay before him at the campsite—evidence that something very bad might have happened. He radioed headquarters, reporting exactly what he had found, and asked for help. Then he started looking for the young woman. "My mind was racing, I was trying to think what was the best course of action," said Marschall. "I'm assuming she's been attacked by a bear, and she could still be alive."

Marschall was torn between a sense of urgency to help a potentially injured person and a feeling of caution. It was the same kind of weird contradiction that circled his head over the tranquil setting of a tent at the edge of a meadow and a piece of human flesh in the grass. An antithesis.

"I started calling her name and started looking up in the woods because about the only way you could go was down to the creek, out into the meadow or up into the woods," said Marschall. "I had known from a lot of previous experience with bears that they usually drag things up hill and into the woods and not out into the meadow. So I started searching around quickly, but still really had the idea that there was a chance that a bear was still there guarding what he considered food and so I was trying to mix caution and speed."

Marschall's radio call came in to the Lake Ranger Station at 11:30 that morning. Within a half hour, a helicopter carrying rangers Dave Spirtes and Tim Blank landed in the open meadow adjacent to the campsite.

Spirtes handed weapons out of the helicopter, keeping a high-powered rifle for himself and giving 12-gauge shotguns to Blank and Marschall. Marschall was glad to holster his .357 revolver, a relatively pathetic weapon when it comes to large animals like grizzlies. Together the three men began to comb the area around the campsite, looking for Brigitta.

The rain from previous nights made the ground hard to read. There were very few tracks. While he had been waiting for assistance, Marschall had found where Brigitta had hung her food between two large lodgepole pine trees, about eighty-five feet uphill and east of her tent. The bear had found the food too. It had climbed one of the trees and broken the thin cord holding the stash. It had then eaten much of the food, biting through some of Brigitta's cooking gear. Marschall showed the damage to Spirtes and Blank, and they swept north and then back toward the ripped tent.

Elsewhere the park swung into action. An emergency medical team stood by at the Lake Hospital, and a search dog team was activated. Sprites requested more personnel. A full-out emergency search was in the offing.

The three men worked back toward the lake, looking for clues. Eventually someone spotted a piece of bloody clothing, some broken twigs, and matted-down grass.

At 12:59, Blank radioed the Lake Ranger Station. The dispatcher noted Blank's orders in the logbook: "Found what we're looking for. Hosp. doesn't need to stand by. Do not (need) dog team. Might need a few more people."

Side-by-side, spaced only a few yards apart, Sprites, Marschall and Blank had followed a barely discernable drag trail. The trail led from the sleeping bag, past a fire ring, across the Astringent-Broad Creek trail, and up into the woods.

"The three of us were walking kind of as a team if you will," said Spirtes. "We had spread out, but we were fairly close together . . . twenty or twenty-five feet apart but we were really on alert."

The trail led from a bloody sweater, to a sock, to a pullover, and finally to Brigitta. She had been dead quite some time. She was lying prone, with her right arm stretched out over her head, her left pinned beneath her body. The bear had eaten much of her body, including almost all of the musculature of her legs, buttocks, torso, and arms.

"I spent a hitch in Viet Nam as a ground-pounder in the 101st Airborne . . . so I've seen bodies before, but at first it just didn't register," said Spirtes. "It was just, here's a body."

"I don't think any of the three of us had ever seen anything like that before," said Marschall. "It was a pretty gruesome sight . . . it just took a minute to gather our thoughts and comprehend . . . . You know, we probably suspected that was the outcome, but just to comprehend the certainness of that, and the finality of that."

The search had now essentially become a homicide investigation, and the helicopter began to shuttle personnel and equipment into the site in an attempt to find out what had happened to 25-year-old Brigitta Fredenhagen on the night of July 30, 1984.

By all accounts, Brigitta was an experienced, "hardy" hiker who wanted to see the Yellowstone backcountry very badly, although she had admitted some trepidation about wild animals. She had flown into the United States from Paris, uniting with her brother and sister-in-law in Denver on July 26. Together, the family drove up to Yellowstone beneath the towering ramparts of the Tetons and entered the park through the south entrance. For a couple of days, they took in the sights of Yellowstone, camping at Grant Village and at Norris. On July 29, Brigitta walked into the Canyon Ranger Station where she was issued a permit to camp at a backcountry site on the night of July 30. Since her brother and sister-in-law didn't have any backpacking equipment, she would be camping alone.

At the station, Ranger Gary Youngblood remembered her as fit, fluent in English, and attractive. She made eye contact, which Youngblood later said was very unusual for most park visitors. She was given all the standard warnings: how to camp in bear country; don't drink the water; put your fires out; and for women, the potential dangers of camping in bear country while menstruating. Brigitta's initial plans called for her to do a lengthy trip, hiking up from Pelican Valley, over into the Broad Creek drainage, and out at Artist Point on the edge of the Grand Canyon of the Yellowstone River.

The Fredenhagens camped that night at Norris, and the next afternoon they hiked into the panorama of Pelican Valley. About five and half miles in, Andreas and his wife, Junko, said goodbye to Brigitta. Before they parted, plans for the longer hike had been scrapped and Brigitta promised to meet Andreas and Junko back at the Pelican Creek trailhead the next afternoon.

Four-and-a-half miles away up in his perch in the Pelican Cone fire lookout, biologist Kerry Gunther trained his 2000 mm telescope on the Fredenhagens as they reached the junction of the Astringent-Broad Creek trail and the main Pelican Valley trail. "I didn't know it at the time," remembered Gunther, "but I saw a group of three people come up, and at the Astringent Creek junction, two of the people had day packs and one person had a big pack. So one went on and the other two turned around."

Brigitta continued up the trail and, whether she decided that she couldn't go on to her assigned site or she was confused about which site was which, she camped at 5W1. It was a campsite that had been used off and on that summer by small parties of between one and three people. Ironically, a group of three German hikers had been assigned to use 5W1 that evening and had even started on the trail. But a mile or two in, the Germans decided they had gotten too late of a start, so they turned around. They visited briefly with Andreas and Junko. Brigitta camped at the spot where they would have been. Her assigned campsite was another three miles up the trail.

From the film in her camera and other evidence, rangers pieced together her journey. Along the way, she stopped and took a few pictures, snapshots of dark forest and brilliant green meadow spattered with yellow wildflowers. At White Lake she set up her tent, staking it tight and pulling the dark green rain fly taut. She took more pictures: of her tent set so perfectly at the edge of the trees only about thirty feet off the trail, of the outlet of White Lake thick with water lilies. She may have eaten dinner, listened to a tape of classical music she had in her tape player, or read a little bit from a guidebook she had packed in. Ranger Mark Marschall wrote that guidebook. As evening approached, she found two large trees away from her tent, climbed them and hung her food, stringing it between the two trees about twelve feet above the ground.

Then she turned in for the night. She neatly folded the clothing she'd been wearing that day, including jeans and a flannel shirt, and placed them in a plastic bag inside her tent. She wrote in her journal that she had taken "all precautions." And then she shut off her flashlight and tucked inside her sleeping bag, zipping it all the way up and fastening the Velcro at the opening.

These actions—the precautions and hard work of a solo hiker trying to keep a clean, perfect camp in bear country—rattled investigators. Brigitta Fredenhagen had done just about everything right, and there was no obvious pointer, no one glaring factor that officials could gesture to and say, "Hey, this is why the bear killed her." She wasn't menstruating, she had put all her food out of reach, and she had even put her clothing in a plastic bag inside the tent. She followed the rules.

There are many reasons that humans get hurt or killed by grizzly bears, but the rarest of all attacks and perhaps the one we fear most, is the bear on the hunt, the bear that comes into a campsite for the sole purpose of hunting a human. This is what apparently happened to Brigitta.

It rained hard that night. Sometime, perhaps during the storm, a grizzly bear entered Brigitta's camp and discovered the food hanging from the tree. Brigitta had hung her food from what wilderness folk call a "ladder tree," a tree that has plenty of branches that make it easy for a human—or a grizzly bear— to climb the tree like a ladder. The bear climbed the northernmost tree, stepping on the branches until it reached the thin, orange, parachute-type cord, apparently swiping at the cord until it broke and the food hit the ground.

Maybe at that moment the rain was drumming hard on the tent fly, or perhaps the sound of thunder or wind rocking through the trees covered up the crash of the food cache. Perhaps Brigitta was tucked deep down into her sleeping bag, warm and snug in the storm, and heard nothing.

The bear ate a little food from the cache, including some

cereal, peaches, and perhaps some smoked ham. It bit the cook pot. Then it made for the tent.

The bear struck quickly, making three swipes. The first hit somewhat to the right of the tent door. The second cut through the rain fly at the door and the third went into the tent itself. By all the evidence, it appeared the bear had pulled Brigitta, sleeping bag and all, out of the tent in one motion so fast that nothing was disturbed inside the tent. There were no signs of a struggle. A report by a board of inquiry noted: "The tidiness of the incident scene seemed almost uncanny."

The investigators theorized that Brigitta had been lying on her right side with her head near the tent door when the bear cut into the tent and pulled her out, either by the left side of her neck or by the top of her head. Six feet from the tent, Brigitta was pulled out of the sleeping bag. Twenty-two feet from the tent, investigators found a large bloodstain where they suspected she died. The autopsy revealed that she had died rather quickly from bleeding and shock.

"It was a surgical strike," said Marschall. "The contents of the tent weren't disturbed . . . it appeared like he reached in exactly where he needed to. It was just kind of amazing predatory behavior by how untentative it was, how direct. It almost seemed like the bear had done it before."

Investigators noted the area was relatively open, not a tight, closed-in pocket where a traveling bear might be forced to walk right by the tent. "I got a spooky feeling there," said Spirtes. "Hey, this wasn't like an accident, this was something where for some reason something set this bear off in this predatory mode and once it got in that mode, you know, a single person in a tent . . . didn't have a chance."

Despite how unusual such attacks are, a similar incident had indeed happened only a year before at Rainbow Point Campground on Hebgen Lake just west of the park. That attack, however, occurred in a developed campground and the bear was quickly captured at the campground and killed. Now the park service had a similar attack except this one was deep in the backcountry, there were a lot of bears around, and the trail was cold. Isolating the bear in question was going to be difficult.

At the Pelican Valley trailhead, a park official met the Fredenhagens and broke the terrible news. The entire valley was closed off while the investigation hit its full stride. More investigators were flown in, and a plan enacted to locate the bear.

Initially, investigators didn't even know the species of the bear that killed Brigitta. Wyoming Game and Fish Department bear biologist Larry Roop found grizzly guard hairs at the autopsy in Cody the next day. Because of the hard rain, investigators didn't find good tracks, and even blood that might have coagulated in clumps had washed away. In all, they found four tracks and one of these was "a front pad 5-1/2 inches wide whose shape suggested a grizzly track," wrote Sprites in his official report.

With years of hindsight, Spirtes noted that the investigators and field team might have done things differently than they did that day in August. They bagged bear scat nearby that they didn't analyze until later, only to find it had human remains. But perhaps more important than anything was the initial attempt to trap the bear.

Because the park helicopter had been used so much shuttling rangers in and out and during a search for another missing hiker in the park, the pilot ran out of permitted flight time. They had to use a helicopter to fly in a trap, and now the pilot couldn't fly because of federal regulations. The trapping effort would have to wait until the next day. Thus, without a trap at the site on the first night after the attack, the best chance to

capture the killer bear was lost. "That may have been the difference," said Marschall. "If the bear came back that night and
found that the body was gone, it is probably not going to come
back in again."

Dave Spirtes had been named operations chief and the pri-
mary investigator. He felt the urgency of the situation. At one
point during the investigation, other rangers turned to Sprites
for advice. "I remember someone saying 'Dave, what do you
think?' and I remember saying this, 'I'm a ranger, I don't think,
I act,'" said Spirtes. "So the dark's closing in, we have got to
decide what we are going to do."

As the very long, very stressful day drew to a close, rangers
were dispatched to a number of locations for the night. The
next day they would come back. That night, Marschall and
fellow ranger Bill Berg went to the Pelican Springs patrol cabin,
while another ranger, Nick Herring, was assigned by himself to
the Fern Lake patrol cabin, only a few miles to the north of the
attack site.

In the hissing lamplight that night, Herring wrote in the
cabin's logbook what every ranger was feeling: "I feel for the
pain she must have felt. What I saw today I will never forget
throughout my entire life . . . The attack on this young lady
was apparently unprovoked. She did everything she was supposed to do to have a reasonably safe camp. She hung her food
correctly, she camped under a tree, she had no food in her tent
with her except a candy bar sealed up inside a backpack which
was undisturbed, she had bear bells for when she was hiking. In
other words she had a good camp . . . Plans for some type of
action are in the working and I will be given my orders in the
morning."

Sometime after midnight, Herring woke to the sounds of
something on the cabin's porch. After listening for a while,
he realized it was a bear. He could hear it snuffling and

scratching on the door, then the windows. He woke, lit a gas lantern, grabbed his shotgun. For several hours the bear tested the door and the boarded-up windows, terrorizing the ranger inside.

The next morning, Herring made this entry: "It was one hell of a long night. A bear made an attempt to get in the cabin last night, I'm guessing around 0130 or 0200 hours. He came up on the front porch and pushed on the front door, then walked around to the east window and pushed on it. I'm really glad I bolted the shutters before retiring to the cabin last evening. I found one real good print in the mud outside the North double window. Looks like it was a grizzly." Later during the investigation, bear scat was found not far from the cabin. The scat contained human remains. Herring reported his harrowing night to the command center, and a culvert bear trap was flown into the cabin and set up.

Armed park rangers fanned out in all directions. The plan was to find bear scat, link that scat to a particular bear if possible, and if the scat tested positive for human remains, identify the offending bear. The technique called for sneaking through the woods, jumping bears from day beds. It was a harrowing duty.

"We are breaking all the rules," said Marschall. "We are trying to surprise a bear. We are going though where we are pretty sure there are going to be bears and we are not making noise. We only surprised one bear off a day bed and that was by ranger Bill Berg and I. That was pretty close to where the incident had taken place, it was on the ridge between Broad Creek and upper Pelican Creek."

The bear was large and probably male and it moved off quickly, not panicking, but putting distance between itself and the men. The two rangers found bear scat nearby and it did have human remains, but they couldn't tie it directly to the bear that fled or to any particular bear. The day was intense. Four pairs of rangers swept through bear country looking for bears, bear tracks, and bear scat.

"It was one of those situations, it was kind of like climbing, I was totally focused on the moment," said Marschall. "There was no thought about anything else but what was right in front of me and deciding if I see a bear, I'm going to do this, and if the bear is doing this, I'll do that and you know, I've got my rifle and I'm ready to fire if the bear does this."

Meanwhile back at the site and in the front country, more measurements were taken, including the width of bite marks on a cooking pot, Brigitta's back, and on her left hand. Mary Meagher, a large mammal ecologist with the Park Service, compared the width of those bite marks to the skulls of grizzly bears at Montana State University in Bozeman. From these measurements and from other clues such as the climbing ability of grizzlies varying with age, Meagher theorized that the offending bear had likely been a male subadult, blondish in color, and not particularly afraid of humans. But other managers theorized that the offending bear was No. 88, a large male that had been in and out of campgrounds for much of its life, an unafraid grizzly that might strike without hesitation in such a situation. Still more people suspected a sow with a cub that had been in the area. All were theories.

As August 2 dimmed, plans were made to set a trap at White Lake. Someone came up with the idea of two traps, one for the bear, another that rangers could squeeze into for protection while they monitored the bear trap. A helicopter brought both traps in.

"I thought this is something only rangers would think of doing, with a combination of what makes sense and just borderline hare-brained," said Marschall. That night he and Spirtes jostled for room inside the bear trap, which was set up perhaps 150 feet from the baited trap.

That night and for several subsequent nights, the baited trap was monitored by two rangers in the other trap. Rangers even went so far as to hang food in the same trees that Brigitta had used. "The bear trap had been set up essentially where her tent had been," said ranger Mike Pflaum. "We tried honestly to recreate the whole scene." It was restless, intense duty, to sleep at a place where a fellow human being had been killed. The bear didn't come back.

"For the remainder of the few weeks that we worked on that investigation, being in the trap turned out to be one of the least scary parts of it, just because going through the woods, looking for these day beds of these bears turned out to be scarier stuff," said Marschall.

The armed hikes were the kind of duty that penetrated the senses and kept everyone on edge. For Marschall and his fellow rangers, it was a good plan, a compromise between shooting every bear they saw and doing absolutely nothing. It was about all they could do in a wild, wide country with bears everywhere. Tracks were measured, bears observed and recorded. Scat collected. From Pelican Cone, Gunther spotted grizzly bears and radioed their locations to the rangers on the ground. The teams would then close in on those bears to try to find a connection between that bear and the bear that had killed Brigitta.

Some officials like Gary Brown, who was the park's bear management specialist, felt a sense of futility. "It was not just that situation," said Brown. "I think in most bear situations there's a certain futility about not knowing what bear (is responsible). Now if you have an incident and there is a radio signal (from a collared grizzly) close by or you have a little suspicion over who it might be . . . ."

At White Lake, they had none of this. They had no forensic evidence to tie the scene to a particular bear, and DNA work was still many years in the future. So the best the investigators could do was what they were doing. An entry in the Fern Lake cabin logbook noted: "No bear last night in either site. All six of us will continue our 'exhaustive search over an area half the size of Rhode Island.'"

Search leader Spirtes penned some of his own thoughts: "As the days go by it will be increasingly more difficult to identify the problem bear. We have hair and measurements from the autopsy but evidence is slow. The question is how can we open the area again without finding the bear? I apologize for the homespun philosophy but I think this incident is making us all look inside ourselves. The mission continues."

On Friday, August 3, good-sized bear tracks were found in the mud near the Pelican Creek trailhead. The front pad tracks measured five and one half inches in width. Scat found on the tracks tested positive for human remains. The tracks were headed out, out toward the developed areas of Yellowstone, toward Fishing Bridge and Canyon and all the places that thousands of tourists visit.

Early in the morning of August 5, the improbable happened. An 11-year old boy at Grant Village, a huge camping complex on the western shore of Yellowstone Lake, was pulled out of his tent and mauled by a bear. It was some thirty-five miles away from White Lake but well within the traveling range of a roaming grizzly bear. The incident was eerily similar to what happened to Brigitta. Could it be the same bear?

Between Grant Village and White Lake lay massive Yellowstone Lake as well as highways and developed campgrounds and thousands of Yellowstone tourists. Could a bear that killed a woman alone in the backcountry one week walk around Yellowstone Lake and attack a camper in a busy developed campground the next week? Most of the people on the investigation thought this was very likely, especially since a powerline provided a good, well-traveled bear corridor between much of the two areas.

"It was so, so similar," said Brown. "We just felt it was the same bear and you tie in the fact that there was the bear scat with human remains down at the Pelican Valley trailhead . . . we don't know for sure. But it sure appeared in our experience, that was the same bear. But we don't know."

"It was the same m.o., the slash in the tent in the same place, the person pulled out," said Brown. "Except at Grant Village the bear got mostly sleeping bag and dragged the bag and the kid fell out."

The kid was Bryan Lynip of Santa Barbara, California. He was less than a month shy of his twelfth birthday. That night, he and his family had gone to an interpretive program held elsewhere in the park and then returned to their campsite late at night. Like Brigitta, the Lynips were meticulous in their camping habits, and they put all of their food into their car. Bryan and his older brother, Keith, slept in a small tent right outside their parents' tent.

Late that night, the bear attempted to bite into a pop-up trailer that was parked in a site nearby, but the screaming of the trailer's occupants apparently scared it away. Then the bear made its way through the campground to the Lynips's campsite.

The bear knocked down some of the tent stakes on the back of the tent. Much of the tent collapsed but not the front. The bear then walked around and made a slash in the front and pulled Bryan out by his right arm. As the bear pulled, it apparently made another bite and came up with nothing but sleeping bag. Bryan fell out of the bag. The grizzly then dragged away the empty sleeping bag.

"The first sensation I had was of being shaken around," said Lynip. "I kind of thought it was a dream. I mean, we had a dog and he used to grab my hand in his mouth and shake my hand around and that's sort of what I thought of, but this was my body being shaken around. The bear had me by my right arm, over the elbow. But I didn't feel a bit of pain. And I kind of came to and realized, this is no dream. I think I went straight from deep sleep into shock, that's why I didn't feel anything."

Sleeping in the tent next door, Bryan's parents first heard a ripping sound and then Bryan yelling, "Daddy, the bear got me. The bear got me!" The entire area then came to life as campers around the Lynips rose and started vehicles. Bryan's father shined a flashlight on Bryan standing outside the tent holding his right arm. His arm was badly lacerated. Bryan was transported to the hospital in Cody for surgery that night. No one, including Bryan, saw the bear, but right away, the investigators had their suspicions.

At the site, Brown and Jerry Mernin, a legendary ranger who had spent his entire career in Yellowstone, found a bloody bear track inside the tent on a foam pad. The track was good enough to confirm it had been a grizzly bear but not good enough for exact measurements to be taken to compare to the tracks at White Lake. There were tracks in the sand along the lake, but they, too, could not be tied directly to the White Lake tracks.

"We had some tracks . . . and they were partial," said Brown. "They really didn't tell us anything."

Mernin measured the bite marks in the pop-up trailer. They differed by only two millimeters from the marks on Brigitta's left hand.

The media went wild. Headlines around the region trumpeted: "Park calm as rangers hunt bear," "Yellowstone bear kills camper," "Park officials report bear ate part of Swiss backpacker," "Grizzly blamed as killer," and "Bear Mauls Youth Sleeping in Tent in Second Attack at Yellowstone." Letter writers called for grizzly bear extermination and bear managers' termination.

Meanwhile, the search continued and officials braced for what might happen next.

Each night, the rangers stationed at patrol cabins around the area would write their thoughts and accounts of the day's search for the offending bear. At Fern Lake, the last pages of a log book that had been used to jot down entries since 1965 was filled with notes on the search for the bear that had killed Brigitta. Someone cracked the seal on a new logbook and jotted a dedication: "This log book is dedicated to the memory of Brigett (sic) Fredenhagen who was killed and partially eaten by a grizzly bear at White Lake on July 30, 1984." Ranger Dave Spirtes then wrote a complete account of the incident in the first few pages of the new logbook.

Time ticked on. Traps were pulled from White Lake and the Fern Lake cabin. After all these days, any bear that would be caught would be incidental, and even if they caught the offending bear, there was no way of proving its guilt. Ironically, despite the fact that several bear traps were placed all over the backcountry and front country, including at Grant Village, no bears were caught.

On Sunday, August 12, two weeks after Brigitta had been killed, a strategy meeting was held. Its members included Brown, Blank, Spirtes, Meagher, and Marschall. They decided to discontinue operations in Pelican Valley. Too much time had passed. Getting the offending bear, proving that it had killed Brigitta, would be impossible.

There were several bears under suspicion, including two subadults that were prowling the area, apparently working as a team. It's not uncommon for young bears that have been pushed away by their mother to stay together for a certain period of time. Meagher had theorized that the bear that had killed Brigitta was a young bear, not unafraid of humans. The bite marks that had been found in the cooking gear at White Lake and on Brigitta's body were consistent with a subadult. Meagher had measured a width between of the lower canines of approximately two inches and noted that "no normal adult grizzly lower jaw is this small."

On at least one occasion, rangers approached a subadult to within forty yards. It was not disturbed. Could this have been the bear? There was just no way of telling.

Then there was bear No. 88, a habitual offender, a bear that had spent its career getting into campground problems at Fishing Bridge. On the evening of August 1, the day that Brigitta's body had been discovered, Herring wrote in the Fern Lake cabin log that "The park bear specialist's (sic) are speculating that the involved bear might be bear No. 88. He had been trapped several times in the past for problems he caused in front country campgrounds and other areas. He has never shown this type of aggression in his past history."

The day after the Pelican Valley operations were suspended, park rangers discovered bear-caused damage in Fishing Bridge campground. Three traps were set. Almost a week later, on August 18, bear No. 88 climbed into one of them. The seven-year old male had been trapped after getting into trouble at Fishing Bridge three previous times, twice in 1982, once in 1983 and finally in 1984. He was euthanized.

Marschall, in his official report of the trapping and field investigation, noted that the bear "weighed approximately 350 pounds, had a large, black bear-like head and dark brown coat. Pad measurements were similar to those of tracks" found at the Pelican Creek trailhead next to the scat with human remains. There is no record that teeth measurements were taken.

During the twenty-four hours before and after Gunther saw Brigitta say goodbye to her family on the trail, he had seen the subadult siblings, a sow with a cub, and a large male bear that he was certain was not No. 88. These bears represented only a fourth of the bears Gunther had observed that summer.

The sow was later removed from the population after she got into trouble near Canyon. That left the subadult siblings and the unknown male. Later that fall, the siblings were trapped and handled in management actions. Meagher noted that, "Neither provided the combination of bite mark/front track size necessary to link a particular bear to Fredenhagen (feet not large enough; teeth close but not matched). This case is closed as far as identification of the bear responsible." Both of these bears, which were tagged No. 113 and No. 114, were later killed; one in a management action and the other likely poached.

"So the only one that we didn't know what happened to was the big male that came down from White Lake (the morning Brigitta's body was found)," said Gunther. However, the narrow bite mark seemed to rule out a large adult bear.

After the Grant Village incident, nothing happened. No bears ripped open tents. No campers were dragged off into the night. Nothing. This made some suspect that the killer bear had died. Others felt differently.

"I was always uneasy. I was always uneasy," said Brown. "I never felt that there was any indication that that bear had been taken and removed. We just didn't know and being we didn't know, I just always wondered. I was never comfortable that that bear wasn't still out there."

Marschall, though, was certain that No. 88 killed Brigitta. "I feel really confident that it was bear 88," said Marschall. "It was a bear that had a long history of being trapped and I really believe that it was a bear that had had a lot of experience around people. This bear was trapped at Fishing Bridge, which is only a short jaunt into Pelican Valley. The fact that it never happened again . . . it was a classic bear that would kill somebody, a big male bear, unafraid of people, and it certainly had the ability to do that. I think that's the bear."

There was never any proof, however. In late August, a board of inquiry convened on Brigitta's death. That board issued a conclusion that Brigitta was killed by "a single subadult (2-3 years of age) grizzly bear."

The board also recommended that "there is need to specifically examine and refine, if necessary, the following areas: 1) better ways to store foods in grizzly country; 2) the proximity of camping sites to trails; 3) proximity of food storage and cooking to sleeping areas; 4) proximity of camping sites to preferred bear habitat; 5) the recommended camping group size in the backcountry; and 6) public awareness of risks when camping in grizzly country."

As a result of these findings, the park service and other agencies looked at a number of camping areas around the backcountry. In the park, the Pelican Valley and White Lake campsites were closed permanently. Bear poles for hanging food were installed at a number of backcountry campsites. Others campsites were moved away from trails, and minimum group sizes were recommended but not mandated.

The White Lake site was what Marschall called a "model for what's wrong in most bear-country campsites. It was right close to the trail, it was right on the edge of a meadow, and near a creek, right along a route of travel for bears. So those make the most enjoyable campsites and the most natural. That's where people are drawn to, but yet that as tranquil as it looked, that was probably a bad spot for a campsite."

But even with these recommendations, some still feel that what Brigitta did or didn't do was not really a factor in her death. She had hung her food from a "ladder tree," "but I can't believe that the food situation really had anything to do with that mauling," said Brown. "I think whether there had been no food at all, that bear was going to do that. She was in the wrong place at the wrong time."

There have been only five bear-caused fatalities in the Yellowstone National Park's history. This is the only case where there wasn't an obvious mistake made by the human that could have led to death.

For Marschall, the Yellowstone backcountry would never be the same after he found Brigitta's body. A career wilderness ranger, he still went into the backcountry often and happily, but the country felt differently from that day on. In 2001, almost twenty years later, he finally left Yellowstone to take a job at Yosemite, a park with plenty of problem black bears but no grizzlies. Brigitta's death stays with him.

"I think a lot of us really believed that tragedy struck people who were doing things wrong," said Marschall. "This really changed that."

Investigation leader Spirtes put it this way on the night of August 4, 1984, in the Fern Lake cabin log:

"Any of us who saw Brigitta Fredenhagen's body or talked with her brother and sister-in-law will never forget. After a few years working in Yellowstone and seeing poached wildlife, the victims of accidents, too many miles on a snowmobile, and too much bureaucracy, one's view of the park changes. It is still perhaps the most amazing and beautiful two and a half million acres on the globe—but somehow a paradise lost."

The bear chasers

*Trying to keep the peace between bears and people in
Wyoming's busy "human-bear interface"*

Houses march to the skyline like fat clouds stacked in a
troubled sky. Everywhere I look, there are houses scattered across
the sage. Here and there, the shine of raw lumber catches my
eye: another one going in. And another. Another. Lower, the
houses are modest, the acreage irrigated and fenced off in small
pastures of five, ten, fifteen acres. But as my eye rises, following
the contours of swelling land, up into the sage, the houses get
bigger, fancier, hand-crafted. Far up on the last skyline before
the beginning of public land, a massive castle of a house sits
overlooking it all. I wonder about the ego in that house, wonder if the people who live there feel lordly, looking down upon
the peasants with their little flocks of sheep, a cow or two, a
barn-sour horse.

There is open space too, long sweeps of it, mostly irrigated,
mostly covered with cows or alfalfa or both. Irrigation pipe angles
south and north, white pipe laid like string across pool table
felt. The ranches are keeping this country open, but every year
a new ranch is "ranchetted," chunked up like cheese, sold, fenced,
housed. This is the Wapiti Valley.

Were it another century, this valley west of Cody might be
covered in bison and antelope, herds of elk up high. There's a
similar valley over a few ridges, back in there, called Lamar.
That valley is full of bison and elk and antelope. Unlike this one
though, the Lamar is in Yellowstone National Park. The Wapiti

is mostly private land, and I find myself thinking, "If only the park makers' pens had slipped a bit farther east."

The Wapiti Valley lies just west of the massive Buffalo Bill reservoir. The valley's high flanks are covered in sage and bunch grass, while the bottoms are strewn with cattle and hay meadows. For decades, the valley was ranch country. There were dude ranches up the North Fork of the Shoshone, and cattle ranches in the lower country. The reservoir drowned a few of them. Today, the rising tide of development is threatening the rest of it.

In the middle of all this, wildlife tries to exist on ground that they have been treading for generations. The valley is critical habitat for elk, deer, and bighorn sheep. Not to mention grizzly bears and black bears.

At the wheel of the big, green F-250 is Mark Bruscino, a biologist, a bear trapper. He shifts the Ford into first gear and steers it up a steep grade. The culvert bear trap rattles behind us. It is empty. Bruscino has pulled the trap. For a few days, it sat in the driveway of a house perched precariously on an open sage hillside that used to be winter range for deer and elk. Now it's a housing development. The owners of that house, an ancient couple who bought their dream patch of sagebrush way back in the 1980s, saw a bear in their yard a few days ago. It was a big bear, a grizzly, and it had its feed-bucket-sized head stuck in a tool shed full of birdseed. The old man, who on a good day has trouble bending down to put on his slippers, shuffled out to within ten yards of the feeding bear and shot a dose of bear spray at its rump. He didn't know if he hit the bear, but it ran off. Then the old man called Bruscino.

"Be careful," said Bruscino. "I'll haul a trap up there and get him out of there."

For three days the trap sat near the shed, guillotine-style door open and ready, with a chunk of road-killed antelope cooking inside in the July sun. The big grizz never came back. Now the trap bounces on its single axle as we haul it to another location. A grizzly, maybe the same one, was seen along the river, walking past the Wapiti Elementary School. The school has a brand-new fence around the playground. Its sole purpose is to keep bears out and kids in.

The radio crackles and a disjointed, flat voice comes on: "GF-61, GF-61."

It's another call for Bruscino. Yet another bear has been reported. This one is at a dude ranch in the Sunlight Basin country. The bear, unknown species, startled one of the women who owns the place. She stepped out of her cabin in the middle of the night and found the bear eating dog food out of a sack on her front porch. The owners should know better; they've owned the place since the 1950s. Bruscino steers the truck north toward the basin, a trip of many miles over twisting mountain roads.

Although Mark Bruscino's job description is several paragraphs long, two words sum it all up: problem bears. All too often, it's Bruscino's job to take out those problem bears and most of the time "take out" means kill.

Bruscino has probably killed more wild bears than any living man of this or the last century. This is not a boast. It's not something he's proud of. In fact—and this is nothing but raw speculation on my part—he might say that it makes him a little sick.

When you ask Bruscino about bear biology and about bear intelligence, and just about bears as bears, he'll break into an animated and easy to understand lecture about how a warm bear den emulates a uterus, how the cubs are born hairless and blind and no bigger than ground squirrel. There's a well-known picture that was published in *Sierra* magazine not long ago of Bruscino holding two very small fuzzy bear cubs that he extracted from a winter den during a hibernation study. The look on his face says it all. He is thinking he has just about the coolest job in the world.

He'll talk about the amazing bond between a mother and cubs, he'll talk about individual bears that he's known, and he'll talk about how bear managers have brought back the wild grizzly in Yellowstone and how that's the major wildlife success story of the last one hundred years. But through it all, there will be just a tint, just a little crack, of sadness. Wildlife biologists don't get into the job for the glory of killing things. They get into it because they care.

Bruscino is a dark-haired man with a big, drooping mustache, dark watery eyes, and a calm voice full of knowledge. He speaks with authority, not condescending like some armchair bureaucrat biologist, but with the kind of know-how that can only come through years in the field, years of tromping through spruce jungles with a radio transmitter to his ear, listening to the steady, bip, bip, bip of a radio-collared grizzly bear. I've sat at his kitchen table and I've eaten at his campfire and I absolutely, unconditionally believe that he knows what he's talking about. Mark Bruscino thinks the Yellowstone grizzly bear is ready to come off the list.

The list, of course, is the endangered species list, the too long and deeply depressing list of animal and plant species that humans have threatened or pushed to the brink of extinction. In 1975 the grizzly bear in the Yellowstone ecosystem was added to the list. It was given the less-ominous status of "threatened," but it was on the list nevertheless.

It was once rare to see grizzlies in Yellowstone, particularly after the sharp declines in the 1970s when the park garbage dumps were closed. But today, biologists like Bruscino and Kerry Gunther, who is the park's chief bear biologist, are seeing bears like never before. Outside the park, bears are now occupying historic ranges they haven't tread in sixty or more years. That keeps Bruscino and Brian DeBolt, his counterpart on the southern end of the wild country, going day after day, chasing down problem bears and educating problem people. Bruscino and DeBolt, as well as other respected scientists like Gunther, think the grizzly has met the recovery goals and is ready to come off the endangered species list.

Others aren't so sure, and they, too, care deeply about the bear. Supported by equally well-respected biologists who have equally impressive amounts of field time, they point to evidence that the grizzly bear is not even close to being ready to come off the list. These are scientists like Dr. Barrie Gilbert, who in 1977 had the better part of his face chewed off by a Yellowstone grizzly bear and who adamantly believes that the grizzly in Wyoming is still in serious trouble.

"There is too little concern for known threats to the future of the major foods and threats of human invasion of their habitat," says Gilbert. "Another way of saying this is, if we have not halted the factors that have caused the decline of bear populations, why would we declare that they are ready for delisting?"

Those who oppose delisting can back up their concerns, and their evidence, admittedly, is much less ephemeral than 500 seldom-seen grizzly bears floating around the ecosystem. Their's is evidence even a layperson can see. It is the line of trophy homes marching up the flanks of Sheep Mountain outside the Wapiti Valley. It's the clot of summer homes in the Little Warm Springs subdivision outside Dubois. It's the blob of highbrow castles choking Spring Creek outside Jackson, and it's any number of developments that have spread into what was once part of northwestern Wyoming's big empty. It's as if Yellowstone National Park and the surrounding wilderness is the last healthy tissue in the body and the encroachment is an ever growing, ever-swallowing cancer.

"Bear numbers are up," says Bruscino as he steers the Ford north to Sunlight Basin and another problem bear. "They've done extremely well, they are inhabiting large areas of the ecosystem. Bears have recolonized areas recently that they haven't been in probably fifty to one hundred years. The new challenge now is managing them in what I call the human-bear interface which is not the wilderness setting, not the park setting, but the setting where bears and humans kind of bump into each other frequently instead of infrequently, including private lands used for livestock production as well as residential areas, including little hobby farms."

Bruscino calls it the "human-bear interface," but perhaps a more accurate term would be the Dead Zone. Bears die here. This loss of wildlife habitat has everyone concerned.

"Development of rural lands into residential areas is not a good thing for long-term bear conservation," says Bruscino. "Bears that frequently interact with people and their property usually end up dead.

"You know a whole host of problems often come along with those rural developments in bear habitat. They often end up being what's commonly referred to amongst biologists as a black hole. A bear gets attracted in there and you kill him. And another bear gets attracted in there and you kill him, and it just becomes a population sink, and that concerns me."

A map showing the location of grizzly bear and human conflicts from 1986 to 2002 says it all. Before 1986, the conflicts were often in the backcountry, close to Yellowstone and Grand Teton national parks, a drop here and there on a wide canvas. Between 1986 and 1995, the conflicts are marked in ever-increasing numbers, spattering out into country as far south as Jackson. Between 1996 and 2002, the droplets become a nearly steady stream, as if a light rain shower has become a downpour. Grizzly-human conflicts have occurred in recent years as far south as the Wyoming Range and as far east as the Owl Creek Mountains outside Thermopolis. Grizzlies have wandered in ever-growing numbers into the northern Wind River Mountains north of Pinedale, and they recolonized the mighty Tetons.

The center of the population is Yellowstone National Park, and as the bear population has grown, younger and less dominant bears have been pushed to the edges, spilling into country that hasn't seen a grizzly in years and into the backyards of newcomers and old timers alike. Grizzlies have been gone from this country so long, that both groups are on the same plateau when it comes to knowledge of how to live in harmony with bears. It's a conservation education nightmare, and someday, someone is going to get killed or seriously injured by a grizzly bear in the low country.

Delisting the grizzly would turn the management of the species back over directly to the states and the national parks. Currently a multi-agency group called the Interagency Grizzly Bear Committee, led by the U.S. Fish and Wildlife Service, oversees grizzly bear management in the Yellowstone region. If grizzlies came off the list, the state wildlife departments of Wyoming, Idaho, and Montana would manage them, and state sportsmen would provide the means. Wyoming sportsmen, for instance, could hunt a few of the bears that Bruscino and DeBolt are now killing themselves.

This makes sense to Bruscino because a grizzly bear hunter could take home a trophy, meat, and a memory, whereas Bruscino himself is injecting a problem bear with a lethal dose of chemical and the carcass goes to waste. The skins from problem bears have sometimes been donated to museums and exhibits for education purposes.

Still, others are concerned about the future of the bear and they point to history. Wyoming and its neighbors are states that are locked in conservative politics, and they fear for the future of the bear in a game where agriculture still is dealt the best hand. But, says Bruscino, the states have worked hard to manage the bear and they aren't going to turn around and lose what they've gained.

"The bottom line is the same agencies who brought the grizzly bear back from the brink of extinction would be the same that would manage the bear if it were off the list," says Bruscino. "But bears need people's acceptance and they need open space, and those things are going to be critical."

Most of the bears that die these days due to "management removal"—which means Bruscino and DeBolt and euthanol— are bears in the Dead Zone. Trash eaters, livestock killers, cabin busters, camp raiders.

In these areas of "human-bear interface," grizzlies often don't last long and it's usually not the fault of the bear. It starts with the human. No bear illustrates that point better than a sow grizzly known as 128.

In 1986, the sow was captured as a nuisance bear snacking on garbage near West Yellowstone, Montana. She was given ear tags, a tattoo, and a number, and she was moved deep inside the park. For several years, not much was heard from her. Then she migrated south out of the park looking, as bears always do, for food.

The country south of Yellowstone is some of the largest designated wilderness in the Lower Forty-Eight. But on the edges, the wilderness falls off into multiple-use country, which means livestock and roads, logging and people. It's still public land, but it's far less pristine than the wilderness itself. Bears don't honor property boundaries. Once 128 was on the edge of public land, she was one step closer to humans. In the fall of 1994, 128 took one too many steps.

That fall her keen nose found the dwelling of one Billy Snodgrass, a man with dreams of winning the Iditarod, the famed sled dog race in Alaska. Snodgrass had a mess of dogs that he was raising for just that purpose, a pack of nearly 100 hungry canines. One big sled dog can eat a lot of food. One hundred sled dogs eat tons of it. Literally. Snodgrass and his wife were caretaking the summer place of a rich absentee landowner on Horse Creek just outside the town of Dubois. When 128 topped a rise on public land, the river of scent wafting up from Snodgrass's kennels must have been the grizzly bear equivalent of hitting the dollar slot jackpot at Vegas.

Snodgrass had tons of dog food stored in a garage. He had a trailer full of trash. His dwelling and outbuildings were the exact opposite of bear proof. So 128 came down the hill and had some fun. She tore into the garage where she found huge, old freezers full of dog food. She opened them and dined away on kibble. The Wyoming Game and Fish Department—Mark Bruscino and Brian DeBolt—were called. They trapped 128 and moved her.

They moved her north, well away from Dubois, and far back into some beautiful bear habitat. The only problem was, a more dominant bear probably already occupied the habitat. Even more important was 128's memory for a meal. She was back at the Snodgrass place the next spring.

"She really became kind of infamous in the Dubois area," says DeBolt. "We set a culvert trap inside this guy's garage where the dog food was and we camouflaged it with these big boxes and kind of made it look like a big cabinet. He had all these old ice machines and these old freezers and that's what he would store the dog food in. She'd come in through the windows.

"The bear had pushed those windows in so many times that those runners had been worn so much that you could literally just touch those windows and they'd fall inside onto his work bench," says DeBolt.

Although Snodgrass didn't really seem to care that he was feeding a bear or two as well as eighty or so sled dogs, it was a problem for his neighbors. They started reporting bear problems, and by the summer of 2001, Horse Creek residents thought the territory was crawling with bears. More likely it was probably almost all 128, who had been positively identified in ten incidents in the area and implicated in thirty-two more. To compound this, she was also teaching her cubs these same habits. An attraction to human dwellings is a deadly attraction, and that year it proved to be deadly for 128.

"We finally caught her in a snare," says DeBolt. "She had gotten into this one particular plastic garbage can time and time and time again that the guy had used to feed his dogs with. There'd always be just a little bit left in the bottom and he had it in his garage. She'd come in and that would be the first thing she'd tip over every time. So we drug it outside and put a snare next to it and sure enough, we caught her right in his driveway, but we didn't catch the cubs, we had some snares and culverts around, but we didn't catch them."

They were young cubs that had been born that winter. When DeBolt drove up and tranquilized their mother, they took off, crossed the creek, and sat up on a hillside. DeBolt pulled the dozing mother into a culvert trap. Then he sat in his truck and waited.

"I tied a rope to the door of the culvert and was just holding onto it inside the truck and mom was asleep inside the culvert," says DeBolt. "So the cubs come running down off the hill and they wanted to be with mom so bad. You know bears have such a tight family group, they just jumped right in that culvert with her, and then I just let go of the rope and shut the door and then I had all three of them."

Under the Endangered Species Act, wild grizzly bears can't go to private facilities such as some educational theme parks located around the country. Zoos are full up with grizzlies as well, and when they do decide they would like to have another bear for their exhibits, they usually opt for a captive-raised bear. Grizzlies are relatively easy to raise in captivity and wild bears sometimes don't adjust well to zoos. In the end, all this means that problem bears often have nowhere to go and end up dead, and it's people like DeBolt and Bruscino who have the unpleasant job of doing the killing.

DeBolt injected all three bears with a lethal dose of euthanol that stopped their hearts. The grizzly bear family was mounted by a taxidermist and put in the Shoshone National Forest office in Dubois. At least, says DeBolt, maybe some good will come out of their deaths since they are in an educational display warning about the problems of feeding bears. As for Snodgrass, he quit the country and took his dogs with him. If another bear moves into the territory, DeBolt hopes landowners have learned from the lesson of 128.

But perhaps not. DeBolt and Bruscino and one or two other employees of the Wyoming Game and Fish Department stay on the run most of the summer. When the bears come out of the den, their phones start to ring. When the bears den up in the fall, their phones stop ringing. In the dry year of 2002, the phones started ringing on February 28 and stopped on November 25. More than 200 of those phone calls were grizzly bear incidents. Many of these calls are routine—come in, try to trap the bear, the bear moves on, pull the trap. Even a successful trapping is usually fairly uneventful, but not always.

Wyoming game warden Brady Vandeberg has a souvenir from one of those non-routine encounters. It's a rubber bullet that he shot at point-blank range into the neck of a sow grizzly that nearly got into the cab of a pickup truck with him.

It started off uneventfully enough. In August 1997 on the west side of the Tetons, only a few miles from the Idaho border, a bear had been preying on domestic sheep. A sow grizzly was quickly caught in a snare, tranquilized, ear tagged, and put into a culvert trap. Bruscino says she was a non-target bear, meaning she wasn't doing the killing; they suspected a black bear was killing the sheep.

Vandeberg was part of the crew that moved the 250-pound bear over the Tetons, deeper into Wyoming. Just south of Yellowstone, they got ready to release her.

They drove down a remote dirt road, blocked the tires of the culvert trap, unhooked it, and got ready to pull up the door of the trap using a rope tied to one of the pickup trucks. Vandeberg and an agent with the federal Wildlife Services sat in another pickup truck twenty yards away. Vandeberg eased himself into position in the passenger seat with a shotgun loaded with five rubber bullets. The idea was to give the bear some fear of humans by whapping it several times on the rump after it came out of the trap.

By this time, the six-year-old sow was wide awake and not very happy. Vandeberg aimed the shotgun out of the pickup window and gave the nod. The second pickup pulled away and the door came up.

"She changed the script in a hurry," says Vandeberg. "While she was only half way out of the trap she turned and looked at me and immediately charged."

He shot her. The rubber bullet bounced off her hide. He shot her again. And again. Still she kept coming, closing the distance between the trap and Vandeberg as fast as he could pump the shotgun. He shot her again. "You can pump four rounds through a shotgun pretty fast."

Rubber bullets are designed to whap a bear fairly hard, and at very close range they are dangerous and can even kill. But nothing fazed the sow. "I don't know exactly where they were hitting but I recall at one point she kind of ducked her head and flinched a little, and I whacked her right in the face with that one and it kind of got her attention, but it didn't slow her down."

Vandeberg thought each shot would be the one that would make her change course and run off into the woods. But in one quick lunge, she came into the window of the pickup truck.

"When she got so close that I couldn't see her, I slid back in a hurry and mashed into the driver," says Vandeberg. "It was kind of instantaneous, and she popped up in the window."

The bear got her front paws on the windowsill and made a lunge to come in. That's when Vandeberg shot her with his fifth and last shot. That bullet, fired only two inches from her neck, merely bounced off her hide into the cab of the pickup truck. "That's unbelievable," says Vandeberg. "It should have killed her."

The sow lunged again, trying to get into the pickup, but Vandeberg held the barrel of the shotgun against her neck, pushing as hard as he could, bracing himself against the driver. The grizzly took huge bites out of the headrest behind the passenger seat while Vandeberg braced himself and pushed with all he had. "It went on for a while because she had time to chew the headrest and just mangle it."

The driver of the truck, an agent with Wildlife Services, pulled his .45 pistol and held it inches from the bear's head, saying, "I'm going to kill her."

But Vandeberg didn't want the bear killed. "I said, 'No, don't, I'm holding her. If she makes another lunge, go ahead, but I'm holding her.'"

The bear was swinging its head from side to side, holding onto the door with both front feet and biting the headrest and anything else it could get in its jaws. In an attempt to scare her off, the driver then shot a round from his .45 right past the bear's ear. Nothing happened.

In the other truck, another Wyoming Game and Fish Department employee was shooting the bear trap with his pistol,
trying to clang the trap and make as much noise as possible.
The bear was completely unfazed. In a third pickup truck, two
U.S. Forest Service employees watched open-mouthed. One of
them had a camera and took a few hasty pictures through the
truck window, but she later told Vandeberg that she stopped
taking pictures because she felt she was going to be taking pictures of their deaths.

Finally, after what seemed like an eon but was probably only
one or two minutes, the bear "finally decided that we had had
enough," says Vandeberg. "She backed out, reached up and bit
the top of the door and put a big ol' gouge in that and then
kinda slid off and chewed her way around the grill, slapping it
and biting it." Then she went to the trap and slapped it and bit
it, and then ran off into the woods.

As soon as she had slid to the ground, the driver started the
truck and backed as quickly as he could out of the area. In
hindsight, Vandeberg says they should have had the truck running so they could have left quickly when the bear made her
move. He also says that maybe they shouldn't have done aversive conditioning—shooting rubber bullets at a bear—in such
a manner in the first place.

"Aversive conditioning is kind of site specific, like if you've
got a bear at a dumpster, you whack them there to teach the
bear to not go into a dumpster, so it really wasn't the appropriate situation, but I guess the thinking was, give her a little fear
of humans, keep her headed away," says Vandeberg.

Apparently the bear went on to a successful life. Shortly after
it was released, it made its way back to Badger Creek. The next
fall her radio signal came from Moose Creek in the Tetons, and
shortly after that, the transmitter failed. "I think she's lived a
long happy life since then," says Vandeberg.

Bruscino has also had a near-miss with a trapped grizzly. We have set up the trap at the dude ranch. It's late evening now and pouring rain, big sheets of it. Bruscino works in the rain, dragging a chunk of antelope from the porch where the dog food was to the trap, leaving a scent trail. He climbs into the trap and sets the door. The door release is tied to the antelope bait; if the bear climbs into the trap and pulls on the bait, the trap door slams down hard and locks. Sometimes, somehow, bears have been able to grab the bait and get out without triggering the door. Other times, Bruscino has found the trap door closed, but no bear in the trap. There's a catch that is supposed to latch and lock the door, but sometimes it fails and the bear lifts the door and gets out.

At the ranch, Bruscino takes the time to lecture some of the guests who are staying there. He tells them about the dangers of going around the trap and about being good campers and visitors in bear country. A large slice of Bruscino's time is spent educating people. Often, the education sticks. He thinks things are getting better, that people are getting wiser, but, he cautions, it only takes one bad camper or cabin owner to habituate a bear, and it's very hard to turn around a bear once it sees humans as a food source.

Bruscino's near-miss came on a grizzly he had snared near Jackson. "It was an adult male grizzly bear that had been killing cattle north of Jackson. We observed it from a distance and could tell that it wasn't caught well. You could see the cable (of the foot snare) and it wasn't around its wrist, it was around the lower end of its foot, which is obviously a concern because you don't want the bear to come out of the snare when you are approaching them."

Almost always, bear biologists tranquilize snared bears by shooting them from a vehicle. But on this bear, the men had to get ten yards closer on foot to be in range of the dart gun.

Bruscino tells the story: "So Chuck Anderson and I got out and the bear was acting real calm. He was just sitting at the base of the tree but he'd lift up his paw occasionally and you could see where the cable was. We approached him and he's still acting real calm, and Chuck had the dart gun and I had the shotgun filled with slugs, and we were shoulder to shoulder which is actually the way we approach the snare because that way it gives the bear almost 360 degrees to run if he comes out.

"So we approached, and that bear was very calm and sitting at the base of the tree where the snare is anchored, so he had a fair amount of slack in the chain. Chuck shot him with a dart in the left shoulder, and he just kind of shook and looked us dead in the eye."

Then he ran all-out for the men.

"He's a big adult male bear and he just ran as hard as he could, just straight at us, and of course (when he reached the end of the chain) that jerked his leg back under him and he flipped over onto his back," says Bruscino. "I didn't even have time to react, I don't think I could have shot him. He came that quick. But the snare held him. I looked at Chuck and his eyes were about as big as saucers and I'm sure I looked the same way. And of course we instantly retreated before the bear got his wits about him and made another charge."

After the bear went under from the drug, Anderson and Bruscino discovered it had only been caught by the front half of its foot, essentially by four toes. "We cabled him to the tree in case he came awake and then we just radio collared him and released him on site."

Bears are very much individuals, just like people. Some avoid people and coexist successfully for years. One of these was the first bear ever trapped by the Wyoming Game and Fish Department, Bear Number One.

When Number One was trapped on Lodgepole Creek just east of Yellowstone, it was 1975 and he and his kind had just that year come under the protection of the Endangered Species Act. Number One would be the first grizzly that Wyoming would study as part of their efforts to recover the grizzly bear population. It was May 21, 1975, and the big male was estimated to weigh just over 300 pounds. During the next two decades, Number One would be trapped six times. Each time, he was weighed and measured and his condition recorded. Except for the radio collaring, Number One lived a life of relative anonymity, eating bear foods and going about his bear business. He was a wilderness grizzly to the core. He spent his whole life—three decades—in the park or in the very remote wilderness at its southern and eastern borders.

On September 23, 1991, Number One stepped into a snare that had been set on the Siggins Fork of Open Creek, far back in the Teton Wilderness in the legendary country called the Thorofare. It would be the last time the old bear was caught.

The trapper, who took meticulous notes on the old bear, was a young man who had grown up in Wyoming. He was an elk hunter, a game warden, a man who had fully embraced the outdoor life. He was twenty-nine years old. Number One was twenty-seven years old, ancient for a grizzly bear, especially in a world full of humans

The big old grizzly weighed more than 500 pounds. He was in relatively good shape and very fat. His teeth were worn and the lower right canine was broken off. He was battle scarred and graying. Although the old bear went into hibernation in fine shape, he died, probably from old age, the next April near Cliff Creek, deep in Yellowstone.

The young man who had trapped him for the last time was

Kirk Inberg. Any book about Wyoming bears would be empty if it left out this man. Inberg, along with fellow biologist Kevin Roy and pilot Ray Austin, were the first grizzly bear researchers to die in Wyoming.

Less than a month after Inberg trapped and examined Number One on Siggins Fork, Inberg boarded a light plane in Jackson along with Roy and Austin. The trio was on a routine flight to see if they could pick up radio signals from collared bears. They left the Jackson airport in the morning and flew to the Grouse Mountain area just outside town in an attempt to locate a grizzly bear that had been shot and wounded by an elk hunter. Later, they swung the plane north to the Thorofare country to locate more radio-collared bears. It may have been a smooth ride that morning, but as October 16, 1991, wore on, conditions got ugly. A forest fire that had been smoldering on Cottonwood Creek outside Jackson blew up in strong winds, and heavy smoke swept across the entire area.

Ironically, Inberg was supposed to return to the airport while Roy and Austin would take off again and go deeper into the country. For some reason, though, he decided to keep on flying. Perhaps he wanted to locate the old bear he had collared a few weeks earlier. Maybe Inberg turned the dial to the frequency of Number One's collar. There were a lot of maybes that day. The only sure thing is that they never returned. The plane went down in some of the most remote country in the Lower 48 states, an area larger than several eastern states combined.

When the plane didn't return that afternoon, a search was launched almost immediately. The search was dubbed High Grizzly, and it became the most massive search in Wyoming history: 150 searchers on the ground, several dog teams, seven helicopters, and thirty airplanes. After two weeks searching

over 2,000 square miles or more, winter swept in and suspended the search.

The next year searchers went back in those woods, looking.
For the next several years, searchers kept looking. The crash hit
everyone hard and everyone looked, combing the seemingly
endless high country whenever the weather permitted. Almost
as soon as the snow melted in the spring, search groups went
into the backcountry. When snow flew in the late fall, they
quit. Every year, the same pattern.

Kirk and Kevin's colleagues at the Wyoming Game and Fish
Department did searches of their own each year using their
own money to spend a week or two in this drainage or that
drainage, always looking always searching. County investigators initiated searches as well, trying to grid search areas sys-
tematically. Kirk's father, Dick, pulled in some volunteers from
his backcountry horsepacking club to do another search. At all
the trailheads leading into the wilderness where the plane had
disappeared, signs were posted with a picture of the blue, orange, and white airplane, a single engine Maule M-5, numbered N19AR. State newspapers did periodic updates on the
search. But as the years rolled by, it looked as if N19AR had
simply disappeared forever—until September 23, 1995, exactly
four years after Inberg had trapped bear Number One.

On that day, Michelle Perry from Thermopolis went elk
hunting. She and her husband and a couple of friends were
camped on the Soda Fork of the Buffalo Fork of the Snake, deep
in the Bridger-Teton National Forest. Above their camp stood a
huge mountain of spruce and rock. It was an unlikely place to
hunt, but she heard a bull elk talking in that timber. Later, off
the mountain, she would shiver with the mystery and coinci-
dence of it all. It was, she said, almost as if the elk were a spirit
calling her up there.

The elk called in that throaty bugle that makes your heart

race and your mouth dry. So Perry climbed the mountain, easing through the timber, hoping to catch a glimpse of him. He bugled and she climbed. Four, five, six hundred feet above camp. He bugled and she took another step, then she saw him and raised her rifle.

After the shot, she took a step toward him and her boot hit something metallic. She had a weird flash of thought that someone was watching her. She immediately thought, "It's the plane." She knew. She knew that the burned timber and twisted metal she was looking at was the plane.

A practical Wyoming woman, Perry field dressed her trophy and then pried off the plane's identification plate. She worked her way back to camp, marking her route. Her husband mounted their best horse and took off for the trailhead some twenty miles away. A phone call later and a chopper was in the air over the crash site. The identification plate proved it. N19AR had been found.

They didn't find much of the men who died in that plane. The pilot, Roy Austin, had been thrown from the wreckage; the bodies of the other two had burned up inside. It appeared as if all three had died on impact. Authorities found Inberg's pistol and belt, nothing else. The fire had been intense and by some twist of fate it had burned quickly and gone out. A few trees had burned, but the fire hadn't spread.

It is a miracle the plane was ever found. I've been to the crash site and it's a benign, nondescript hillside of dark Englemann spruce. There are swales and dips large enough to hide houses. The forest is thick and clinging and when you are up there you think about jumping grizzly bears out of their day beds.

Several summers after the discovery, Bruscino and several other Wyoming Game and Fish Department employees took Kirk's parents, Dick and Judy, to the crash site. Along on the trip was Kirk's dog, Hap, a red heeler that was getting up in years. At the site, they nailed a plaque onto one of the nearby trees. It read:

The Final Resting Place.

At this location on October 16th, 1991, three dedicated men lost their lives to ensure that grizzly bears would always have a place in the heart of the Yellowstone country. Wyoming Game and Fish Department employees Kirk Inberg, Kevin Roy, and their pilot, Ray Austin, braved the uncertainty of fall weather in the Rockies to track radio collared bears so that information could be obtained to guarantee the survival of the grizzly. This location marks their final resting place. Kirk, Kevin and Roy will forever walk these mountains with the great bear.

A picture of that plaque sits in a photo album on the coffee table in Bruscino's house. There are other pictures of that day too. One of the pictures is of Bruscino staring at something on the charred trunk of a standing dead tree near the twisted skeleton of the plane. It's not a very good picture, but if you look close, you can see what is capturing Bruscino's attention: grizzly bear claw marks. Five long scratches in fire-blackened wood.

For three days, I rattle around in the pickup with Bruscino, following up this bear report and that bear report. My maiden bear-trapping voyage ends without a bear. After a few days, Bruscino returns to the dude ranch on Sunlight and pulls the trap. The bear never came back and Bruscino needs the trap. He has another call. It's down in the Greybull River country. A bear is causing some problems.

Epilogue: Like flying salmon

It is late July. Timberline. High up in steep rugged country, doctoral student Hillary Robison focuses her spotting scope and watches grizzly bears. Seven of them. They stand like furry tripods, sprawled out on three feet. Digging with the fourth. Digging for moths.

Every summer, these moths invade our homes. We call them millers and squash them with rolled up magazines. To us, they are house pests, an annoyance. But to grizzlies, grizzlies in tall wild country, they are like flying salmon.

Each summer army cutworm moths fly to talus slopes on tall mountains where they burrow into dark crevices, away from the intense mountain sunlight. Thousands and thousands and thousands of moths. They migrate to the high country from farmland far away, much like salmon migrate from oceans to rivers.

At these places of slide rock and sunshine, the bears also gather, climbing high above timberline and feeding on the moths. Digging and feeding, digging and feeding. With its high fat content, a single moth may account for as much as half a calorie. It is estimated that a grizzly bear may consume some 40,000 moths per day. That means 20,000 calories per day for a talus-pawing grizzly bear. Moths are crucial grizzly bear food.

"If they are spending a month up at these moth sites in the summer, they could eat close to half their (caloric) needs for the year," said Robison.

Robison camps in the high country each summer and eases into an observation point each morning. She's seen incredible things: two sows with a total of five cubs all feeding together; another sow leading her infant cubs on a sliding, tumbling, rollicking glissade down a steep ski-run of a snow field; a pair of grizzlies mating; ten bears all in one place; a brave black bear feeding on a talus slope that had been used by grizzlies only a short time before. She spends her entire summer in grizzly country, all summer within sight and sound of what some people think is the most dangerous animal on the planet. No grizzly bears have ever come into Robison's camp. No grizzly bears have ever charged her. She's only seen one that was even close enough to charge—about seventy-five yards out—and when she saw it again, it was a mile away and still running.

They are wild bears, repeating an age-old tradition that their kind has known for generations. Up here, eating moths from rocky slopes in the Rocky Mountains. Up here, away from people, away from livestock, away from bird feeders and elk gut piles, away from trash cans and apple orchards. Wild.

Nowhere is the interconnectedness of life so represented than on these wild mountain slopes. Each summer the moths migrate from perhaps as far as 300 miles away. Each year, they hide from daylight in the same rocky, mountain slopes, and each year, the grizzlies return to dig and eat.

Using DNA, Robison is trying to find out if certain moths come from certain areas and return to the same piece of high country every year. If this is the case, perhaps grizzly bear managers can work to save habitat used by moths at other times of the year because it is a crucial link to grizzly bear health in the Yellowstone area. Farmland lost to development outside Bozeman, Montana, or even North Platte, Nebraska, could impact grizzly bears in Yellowstone's backcountry. Spray pesticides in Nebraska or in Wyoming's Big Horn Basin and a whole crop of grizzly food could be destroyed. It is a simple lesson: what we do anywhere on this planet may have consequences elsewhere. Everything is connected.

Grizzly and black bears capture our souls. Their images paint the canvases of our lives. They are individual and they are special.

Up in the Wyoming high country, a wild grizzly paws through a rocky talus slope, searching for food. Down in the low country, I catch yet another miller moth in my house and I carry it outside.

"Go feed a grizzly," I say as I toss it into the Wyoming wind.

About the author

Wilderness trips, bird dogs, and drift boats occupy Tom Reed's time when he's not writing about wild things and wild places. Formerly a resident of Laramie, Wyoming, he now lives in the mountains outside Bozeman, Montana, where he works on public lands issues for Trout Unlimited.

ALSO BY TOM REED
Give Me Mountains For My Horses

Riverbend Publishing
ISBN 1-931832-63-3
$9.95

Tom Reed has a real affinity for horses and wilderness, and it shows on every page in his true tales about trail riding, horse packing, and great mountain horses. Horse lovers will love this book, but Tom's writing is transcendent. Even if you have never saddled up, you will be drawn into these captivating stories of special horses, their remarkable abilities, and the inescapable bonds that develop between horses and humans.

BEARS AND BEARS AND BEARS!

Available from Riverbend Publishing

HIKING WITH GRIZZLIES: LESSONS LEARNED
By Tim Rubbert
This book uses photographs of the author's actual bear encounters to dramatically illustrate how to react safely if you meet a bear on the trail. Each encounter teaches important hiking strategies and gives hikers more confidence to enjoy bear country.

"If you are planning to hike through the wilderness, give this book a careful reading—it could very well save your life." —*Midwest Book Review*

"This book is like a first-aid manual for travel in bear country. It could be the best $10.95 you ever spend." —*North American Bear Foundation*

BEARS I HAVE KNOWN
By Bob Murphy
A former park ranger relates his most memorable experiences with bears. These first-hand stories are great entertainment and an inside look at bear management in our national parks. "This is not your average bear book. It's a lifetime's experience in bear country." – *Bozeman Daily Chronicle*

GREAT WYOMING BEAR STORIES
By Tom Reed
The first-ever collection of the best bear tales from all across Wyoming, including Yellowstone and Grand Teton national parks. "An immensely valuable book for understanding and living with Wyoming's bears." —*Laramie Daily Boomerang*

GREAT MONTANA BEAR STORIES
By Ben Long
Maulings, close calls, and even humorous escapades are all found in these stories, complete with discussions about how to hike, camp, and live safely in bear country. "A must-read for all lovers of wilderness." —*Missoulian*